Comunidad Letrada, Lettered Community

Comunidad Letrada, Lettered Community
Alternative and Independent Publishing in Latin America

Edited by
Marc Delcan, David Woken, and Lisa Gardinier

Litwin Books
Sacramento, CA

Copyright 2025

Published in 2025 by Litwin Books.

Litwin Books
PO Box 188784
Sacramento, CA 95818

http://litwinbooks.com/

This book is printed on acid-free paper.

Publisher's Cataloging in Publication
    Names: Delcan, Marc, editor. | Woken, David, editor. | Gardinier, Lisa, editor.
    Title: Comunidad letrada, lettered community : alternative and independent publishing in Latin
        America / edited by Marc Delcan, David Woken, and Lisa Gardinier.
    Description: Sacramento, CA : Litwin Books, 2025. | Includes bibliographical references and index.
    Identifiers: LCCN2025930408 | ISBN 9781634001441 (acid-free paper)
    Subjects: LCSH: Publishers and publishing – Latin America. | Publishers and publishing – Social aspects –
        Latin America. | Book industries and trade – Latin America. | Small presses – Latin America. | Cartonera
        books – Publishing – Social aspects – Latin America.
    Classification: LCC Z490.C66 2025 | DDC 0270.5098--dc23
    LC record available at https://lccn.loc.gov/2025930408

Contents

1   **Introduction**
            David Woken

Prelude

13   **The Act of Reading is Immersed in a Net Woven by Colonialism**
            Yásnaya Aguilar Gil

Industrial Publishing

21   **How to Prepare Yourself for the Collapse of the Industrial Publishing System**
            Eric Schierloh

27   **The Imperfect Edition**
            Daniel Badenes

49   **Collaborative Distribution: Contingent Alliances and Consolidated Projects**
            Gustavo Velázquez

63   **What is an Independent Publisher?**
            La Furia del Libro

Otras Formas: Case Studies

67   **Queering Digital Publishing: Publishing Practices by Puntos Suspensivos**
            gaita nihil

71	**Breaking Through the Heteropatriarchal Barriers: Rebel Publishing Paths** Rosa Serna
85	**Independent Publishers of the Editorial Market of the City of Belo Horizonte, Brazil** Terezinha de Fátima Carvalho de Souza
97	**The Power of Social and Cultural Capital: Investing in 21st Century Learners Through Access to Latin American Indigenous Works** Kathia Salomé Ibacache Oliva

Artisanal Publishing

113	**Malha Fina Cartonera: Trajectory and Itineraries of an Alternative Model for Publishing** Idalia Morejón Arnaiz, Pacelli Dias Alves de Sousa, and Chayenne Orru Mubarack
139	**The Artist Book in Latin America: Publishing Practice Within and Without the Archive** Peter Tanner, Ph.D.
165	**Scholastic Cartonera Publishers as a Way of Constructing and Promoting the Concept of Bibliodiversity in the Classroom** María José Montezuma Jaramillo

Epilogue

185	**Symbols and Narratives in the Public Space: Other Publishing Fields** E Tonatiuh Trejo

197	**Agradecimientos**
199	**Contributor Bios**
205	**Index**

Introduction

David Woken

This book is for librarians in the English-speaking world who are interested in exploring Latin American materials produced beyond the bounds of major mainstream publishers. Those accustomed to library acquisitions in the Anglophone world often find Latin American markets difficult to understand. The fragmented nature of those markets makes it difficult for librarians to find materials beyond the most famous canonical writers and mass publishers, and in particular skews acquisitions away from works that express the immense cultural, intellectual, and linguistic diversity found in the region. This book is not meant to be a comprehensive guide, nor do we, the editors, believe such a guide would be possible (or, frankly, desirable), but rather an entry point into the constantly evolving and shifting world of alternative publishers, and, as such, a tool for librarians in the Global North to begin to approach the immense diversity of works being produced outside of mainstream publishers in Latin America.

This work is an intervention for those looking to expand their libraries' holdings of materials from Latin America. We have chosen to focus on the "alternative" press in Latin America, works which can easily be missed by librarians looking to increase their holdings in Latin American materials quickly. Publishing markets in Latin America tend to be limited to specific national boundaries with little trade across borders, and are consolidated into a few mega-publishers with state agencies, ministries of culture, and educational institutions taking up much of the rest of the space. While these publishers do provide much excellent material for libraries, their nature as large-scale hegemonic institutions means that they too often reproduce local hierarchies of race, class, and gender in the communities or perspectives they represent.

Our focus is on publishers that operate at the margins of that hegemonic industry, are driven by a commitment to their communities, artistic creativity, or political causes, and that struggle against commercial market imperatives to ensure that alternative voices are heard.

Our focus on small alternative publishers is in part a response to the stated interest in fostering diversity, equity, and inclusion (DEI) in North American academic libraries. It was sparked by a range of developments, including the growing cultural and demographic diversity of communities in the Global North, the desire among academics to address the roles their organizations have played in contributing to systems of colonial exploitation and oppression, and direct response to demands from subaltern communities for recognition, as well as the repair of historic and ongoing oppression, especially the demands for racial justice articulated in the Black Lives Matter movement, Indigenous peoples' demands for decolonization of relations with states descended from European empire and sovereignty over their lands and culture, feminist struggles against patriarchy, and LGBTQI+ demands for dignity, respect, and even basic survival. As eager as North American librarians have been to serve the needs of all members of their communities and redress harms perpetuated by their own institutions, the means to address these questions have been far from obvious. Often the impulse is to consider Latin American materials of any type as addressing demands for greater diversity, equity, and inclusion, without understanding how hierarchies of power play out within Latin American cultures, and how major publishers reproduce those power relations. Alternative presses consciously voice perspectives from communities that have been or continue to be marginalized, allowing library patrons access to a richer panorama of experience than would be available through the monoculture represented by more prominent publishers.

This book is structured around the following broad areas of interest: academic studies of the diverse practices of alternative publishers; testimonies, manifestoes, and reflective essays from authors and publishers within the broad networks of Latin American alternative presses explaining their motives for publishing outside of traditional commercial networks and the practices they use to carve out spaces for the communities they represent, and practical applications for teaching and research that librarians undertake using works from Latin America's alternative presses. We do this for two reasons: first, to address the practical questions librarians may have about how engaging with Latin American alternative presses can address their needs and those of their patrons, but secondly, and more foundationally, to help librarians better understand the praxis of Latin American alternative presses. The publishers highlighted within this work all operate with some degree of ambivalence if not outright hostility toward the market imperatives that drive much of modern publishing, whether due to those imperatives' tendency to homogenize culture around products that appeal to the largest reading public (which is to say, usually white, relatively wealthy, and well-educated populations), their marginalization of materials outside of hegemonic national cultures (silencing Indigenous, afro-descendant, queer, and other marginalized communities), or their role as an element of capitalist exploitation, cultural appropriation, and colonial knowledge extraction. By bringing together publishers, writers, and librarians, we hope this book can be an opening to build relationships that allow us to collaborate in ways that undermine the ongoing colonial practices of Global North knowledge extraction from communities in the Global South and build more collaborative, egalitarian, and reciprocal relationships.

To understand this market-skeptical orientation and distrust of established markets we need an understanding of the basic landscape of Latin American publishing and how it silences those voices outside of hegemonic norms. By "silence" we draw upon the work of Haitian anthropologist and historian Michel-Rolph Trouillot, who drew attention to the active, material role of record making and narrative creation in the silencing of historical voices that clash with those of the powerful. The acts of 1) creating the texts that form the record of our histories and cultures, 2) deciding which of those texts are worthy of preservation in our libraries and archives, 3) determining which narratives of events or cultures are considered valid, and 4) crystalizing those sources and narratives into the master narratives of history all involve acts of silencing certain perspectives while ratifying others as the proper bases of "truth."[1] It is those first two moments of silencing, the decisions about which sources we create and, especially as librarians, which we decide are legitimate to preserve, that are particularly relevant to librarians reading this book. These silences also compound each other. Within the North American academy, perspectives outside of canonical "western civilization" still struggle for recognition and

---

1   Michel-Rolph Trouillot, *Silencing the Past: Power and the Production of History* (Boston: Beacon Press, 2015, 26).

engagement. Latin American perspectives (as well as those from other regions in the Global South) are marginalized further as foreign and, in regard to poorer countries, deemed less important to world historical processes.[2] Within that already limited field of library materials from the Global South, those who struggle outside of or against hegemonic national cultures are silenced further.[3] While we welcome the good-faith efforts of librarians to "decolonize" their library practices and combat the racist legacies of their institutions, one basic but essential element of that process is to seek out the voices of those being silenced.[4]

---

2   Library shifts to prioritizing digital publications in response to the COVID-19 pandemic led librarians working in area studies to speak out about the ways that high level library collection development strategies risked harming the diversity of their libraries' collections, beginning among the Latin Americanist librarians of the Seminar on the Acquisition of Latin American Library Materials (SALALM) Collection Development and Equity in the Time of Covid-19 Task Force "SALALM Resolution: Collection Development in the Time of Covid-19," Seminar on the Acquisition of Latin American Library Materials, June 10, 2020 https://salalm.org/salalm-resolution-collection-development-in-the-time-of-covid-19/. See also ASEEES CLIR "ASEEES CLIR Statement on Collection Development in the Time of COVID-19," Association for Slavic, East European and Eurasian Studies Committee on Library and Information Resources, July 2020 https://sites.google.com/site/aseeesclir/; Committee on Research Materials on Southeast Asia (CORMOSEA) "CORMOSEA Statement on Collection Development, Access, and Equity in the Time of COVID-19," Accessed October 13, 2020 https://cormosea.files.wordpress.com/2020/09/cormosea-statement-on-collection-development-2.pdf; Committee on South Asian Libraries and Documentation (CONSALD) "CONSALD Statement on Collection Development, Access, and Equity in the Time of COVID-19," CONSALD, July 17, 2020 http://www.consald.org/covid.html; Middle East Librarians Association (MELA) "MELA Statement on Collection Development, Access, and Equity in the Time of COVID-19," Middle East Librarians Association (blog), June 22, 2020 https://www.mela.us/2020/06/22/mela-statement-on-collection-development-access-and-equity-in-the-time-of-covid-19/; Joint Area Studies Task Force, "Equity and Access in Higher Education and Academic Libraries Amid the COVID-19 Pandemic," July 31, 2020 https://www.eastasianlib.org/newsite/wp-content/uploads/2020/08/Equity-and-Access-in-Higher-Education-and-Academic-Libraries-Final-August-17.pdf. More general U.S.-based academic library associations responded to these concerns as well; see the Association of College and Research Libraries (ACRL) "ACRL Statement on Equity, Diversity, Inclusion, and the Print Collecting Imperative," accessed October 13, 2020 http://www.ala.org/acrl/sites/ala.org.acrl/files/content/acrlissues/ACRL_Print_Collecting_Statement.pdf; and the Center for Research Libraries Global Resources Network "European Studies Statement on Collection Development, Access, and Equity in the Time of COVID-19, Issued by CIFNAL, GNARP, and SEEMP," August 20, 2020 https://www.crl.edu/news/european-studies-statement-collection-development-access-and-equity-time-covid-19-issued-cifnal

3   This is a process directly analogous to one Trouillot lays out in two chapters, first emphasizing how the Haitian Revolution has been marginalized in world histories of revolutions, and second in the ways that certain factions and leaders of Haitian revolutionaries themselves (particularly the general Sans Souci) have received little attention in comparison to those associated with the ultimately victorious factions in the revolution. See Trouillot *Silencing the Past*, 31-107.

4   We follow the classic statement on the need to make decolonizing interventions of intellectuals concrete and embedded within decolonizing movements put forth by Eve Tuck and K. Wayne Yang, "Decolonization Is Not a Metaphor," *Decolonization: Indigeneity, Education & Society*, 1(1) (September 8, 2012): 1–40.

Latin American publishing markets operate differently than those in the Global North. Literacy levels historically have been quite low, limited to religious, political, and economic elites under Spanish and Portuguese colonial rule and, post-independence, still largely confined to relatively limited privileged classes until well into the 20th century. Publishers, in turn, reflected this reality, publishing under strict supervision by the Catholic Church and the colonial state before independence, and focusing on works by and for a relatively narrow lettered segment of the population who dominated post-colonial political, social, and economic life. It is this long legacy of literacy being intertwined with colonial and postcolonial state and cultural power that led the celebrated Uruguayan scholar and critic Ángel Rama to coin the term "the lettered city" to describe this confluence of power and literacy concentrated in relatively urban political and cultural centers that has characterized Latin America since colonization began in the late 15th century.[5]

By way of contrast, the publishers highlighted in this volume, and the cultural movement(s) of which they are part,[6] are in many ways a counter to the elite monopoly on reading, writing, and especially publishing that characterized much of the history of Latin America. Today the technologies of literacy are much more democratically distributed, but publishing remains relatively restricted. Though no longer constrained by explicit colonial policies to support specific configurations of religious, economic, and racial hierarchy, the Latin American publishing market in many ways reproduces these legacies. However, publishers have found the means to exist and, in many cases, to thrive at the margins of this crowded publishing market, and often follow logics that are in contradiction with, if not outright hostile to, the profit-making imperatives of the market. As you will see in many of the publishers' and authors' statements within this volume, many are driven by the need to provide a voice for their communities, whether those be queer, Indigenous, afro-descendant, or otherwise marginalized by the hegemonic cultures of their nations; others are explicitly political, advancing radical political perspectives from feminist, queer liberationist, decolonizing, or more traditionally leftist communist or anarchist

---

5 Ángel Rama, *The Lettered City* (Durham: Duke University Press, 1996).

6 See Magalí Rabasa, *The Book in Movement: Autonomous Politics & the Lettered City Underground* (Pittsburgh: University of Pittsburgh Press, 2019) on the "organic" book embedded within social movements.

perspectives that find little purchase in mainstream publishing; and many, even when not explicitly political, focus on specific formats, such as artist books, zines, or recycled cardboard *cartonera* books, or aim at specific audiences not served by the mainstream publishing market. And of course, as will be evident after reading the book, many publishers combine multiple of these ideas. In all cases the alternative publishers, authors, and distributors profiled in this book emphasize cultural and political autonomy and service to their communities over the need to pursue profit. In a process that will be recognizable to many librarians who have engaged with DIY publishing and distribution in the North, these publishers rely on a mixture of trade and barter among each other (often across national boundaries), self-driven marketing direct to stores, limited distribution or co-publishing with more mainstream organizations (including university presses, government agencies, and some of the Latin American vendors that U.S. libraries purchase from), and especially the regional, national, and international book fairs that still provide much of the marketing and networking infrastructure Latin American publishing uses to distribute their materials. This constant hustle has been described by the Argentine scholars of modern independent publishing Daniel Badenes and Verónica Stedile Luna as a "permanent state of fairs,"[7] cheekily riffing on the "permanent state of siege" language used by many Latin American military dictatorships across the decades to describe the imposition of permanent martial law. Struggling to spread the word outside of monopoly publishing and distribution markets, the alternative publishers we profile and their comrades have built up their own networks to ensure that the voices they care for are heard despite the lack of interest from the mainstream publishing market.

We organized our book into three thematic sections to help readers to navigate the multiple facets of the subject—Industrial Publishing, Otras Formas: Case Studies, and Artisanal Publishing—but before these we begin with an essay by Yásnaya Aguilar Gil that explores the contradictions of reading and print culture in Latin America. Aguilar Gil recognizes both the knowledge gained and passed on through reading and the simple pleasure that reading can bring, but also the ways that publishing and even literacy itself have privileged colonizing cultures

---

7   "Estado de feria permanente," see Daniel Badenes and Verónica Stedile Luna, eds. *Estado de feria permanente: La experiencia de las editoriales independientes argentinas*, 2001-2020 (La Plata: Club Hem, 2019).

and are embedded in (which is also to say, reinforcing) colonial relations of power that continue to hold Indigenous peoples in subordination and deny the validity of the various ways of knowing and learning practiced by the Indigenous peoples of the Americas.

The section titled Industrial Publishing lays out the broad outlines of the publishing industry in Latin America and independent publishers' place within it, with all authors referring to the sense of crisis that pervades Latin American publishing. Eric Schierloh opens with an essay considering the steps necessary to establish independent presses as a means to survive a kind of ongoing cultural apocalypse of publisher consolidation and consequent cultural homogenization. We follow with translations of two essays from the collection *Estado de feria permanente*,[8] produced by the scholars from the "La edición en la era de las redes" (publishing in the time of networks) project in Argentina's University of Quilmes: Daniel Badenes's overview of the publishing market in his home country of Argentina (and the politics of independent publishing within that market) and Gustavo Velázquez's description of the forms of collaboration, cooperation, and trade among independent authors, publishers, and distributors working to spread their work outside of or in spite of the limits of their local markets. We then end with the manifesto of the organizers of Chile's Furia del Libro, an independent book fair that operates as an alternative to the much larger, more official Feria del Libro.[9] Informal and semi-formal agreements and exchanges, especially those around book fairs (local, regional, national, or international), are one of the primary means for distributing alternative literature, skirting the highly centralized and consolidated publishers and distributors that dominate the publishing markets across Latin America.

Otras Formas: Case Studies follows with three different perspectives on the particulars of individual independent publishers. gaita nihil and Rosa Serna lay out their cases for independent DIY publishing as a means to express the needs of queer (especially elder queer) communities and feminist movements, respectively. What then follows is Terezinha de Fátima Carvalho de Souza's study of one geographically contained publishing market, that in Belo Horizonte, Minas Gerais,

---

8   Ibid.

9   The name "Furia del Libro" (Fury of Books) is a pun on "feria del libro" (book fair), reflecting the countercultural, punky attitude of many of these publishers.

Brazil. In all three cases we see both how independent publishers work to distribute information not favored by the editorial policies of major publishers and how the material practices of writing, publishing, and distributing books are central to their posture before the market and their ability to present their perspectives on their own terms. We then finish with a practical case study from Kathia Ibacache about how independent publishers can be used in library instruction to center Indigenous voices and challenge hegemonic understandings of Latin American culture.

The last section, Artisanal Publishing, focuses specifically on the phenomenon of *cartonera* publishing, a form of publication that emerged from Latin America over the past two decades. Generally attributed to the work of Eloísa Cartonera in Buenos Aires after the economic collapse of 2001, *cartoneras* exist at the crossroads of fanzines, chapbooks, and artist books, with strong social commitments being central to the various publishers. *Cartonera* publishers purchase cardboard ("*cartón*" in Spanish) from scavengers at above-market prices, then use that cardboard to make individually hand-decorated covers for short works (usually offset printed like a zine) that they paste into the covers. The publishers generally emphasize specific communities (around sexuality, language, racial or ethnic groups, etc.), political commitments (usually some form of radical autonomist leftism), or a commitment to artistic and literary expression, but always emphasize affordability and ease of distribution. Though frequently beautiful works in and of themselves, *cartonera* books are meant to be sold cheaply and distributed widely. The phenomenon has spread to all countries in Latin America and many countries elsewhere, including in Western Europe, Sub-Saharan Africa, and North America, but it remains strongest in Latin America. Here representatives of *cartonera* projects explain their commitments and work. Malha Fina Cartonera in São Paulo, Brazil is an extension project linked to the Department of Philosophy, Letters, and Social Sciences at the University of São Paulo dedicated to distributing affordable texts in the city. Peter Tanner follows with a discussion on the larger phenomenon of Latin American artist books. While more specifically a form of individual work of art than the *cartonera*, this essay reminds us that autonomous publication is an outlet for creative expression that does not fit within the publishing market, and provides a medium for cultural experimentation in many forms through the medium of books. The section then concludes on the opposite side of the continent, where María

José Montezuma Jaramillo describes how Ingeniosa Cartonera in Lima, Peru operates as a source of affordable literacy instruction materials for Peru's schools, providing an important resource in a country with staggeringly low reading rates.

We conclude the book with an essay from Oaxaca, Mexico author E Tonatiuh Trejo about reading and publishing as part of the landscape of his city. It is another invitation for our readers to look at their collections beyond the lists produced by publishers and the instrumental demands of our institutions and their curricula. By recognizing the ways in which alternative publishers challenge the social, political, and economic strictures of the market, librarians will not only better serve their patrons, but also will hopefully be closer to being able to understand and navigate the alternative circuits through which so many Latin American perspectives travel.

Prelude

The Act of Reading is Immersed in a Net Woven by Colonialism

Yásnaya Aguilar Gil

Translated by Paloma Celis Carbajal

> Translated from the Spanish *Un nosotrxs sin estado* (Valencia-Chiapas: Ediciones OnA, 2018).

A Gilucho, tyoskujuyëp, amuum tu'uk joojt

I would be lying if I said that I've always enjoyed reading. Before learning how to read, I first learned how to decode the phonetic values of a language that I didn't speak. The clusters of letters that formed texts had no meaning to me and yet made interesting acoustic constructions. The texts had an acoustic body with no semiotic skeleton. As it happened with (I dare to say) all Indigenous peoples in Mexico, literacy arrived in my own town accompanied by a frightening Hispanizing project. It took place mainly during the first half of the 20th century. Literacy was strongly related to the objective of erasing our languages. Promoting literacy meant that the "national" language should triumph over the so-called "dialects," which only meant poverty and backwardness in the thinking of official rural educators such as Rafael Ramírez. Literacy, in my context, was a bet with loaded dice.

I'm aware that underlying within all my reading acts, there is a constant contradiction. On the one hand, reading is an enjoyable act from which I've gained new knowledge and enjoyed multiple aesthetic experiences. But, on the other hand, it evidences the triumph of an imposition during which my mother, my uncles, and I received physical punishment. We did not learn Spanish through some second language acquisition methodology, we learned it through learning how to read in that language.

Reading, always in Spanish, meant, sometimes very obviously and sometimes subtly, that we were denied the possibility, to the point that we shouldn't dare to even think about reading in Mixe, our mother tongue.

Before I dove into the rigors of formal education, I learned to read, at least a part of what is considered the act of reading, guided by my Uncle Genaro. I was raised in a unique environment in which my grandparents and uncles (who were more like my brothers) were excited about communism and the USSR. I owe my given name, a Russian toponym, to the eldest of my uncles. I do not know how, but my hometown of Ayutla, located in the Mixe region of the northern mountains of Oaxaca, received the popular *Sputnik* magazine. My mom and uncles read enthusiastically about Russian factories that held chess tournaments, offered courses in physics or art workshops to their workers, where people were equal, where everything was better than here. And where, if I tried hard enough, one day I could go study.

I'm the second generation in my family who graduated from elementary school. My grandfather attended up to second grade. What he learned allowed him to offer his services as a scribe in addition to tending his land and working in construction. When needed, he would help other people with their correspondence by reading the letters that people in my community received and translating them to Mixe. He would then listen to their replies, translate them into Spanish, and would finally write the answer in a beautiful handwriting that I have never been able to emulate.

My uncles had the opportunity to leave our town to continue their studies. The discrimination they experienced made it clear to them that if I were to learn to read Spanish, I would need to learn how to read without the accent of a Mixe speaker.

Their solution was to teach me how to read before I started elementary school, in other words, before I was taught to speak Spanish. They were not interested in teaching me to speak that language, they wanted me to learn to read it. They were convinced that, to have a strong foundation in Mixe, I had to grow up as a monolingual girl but, paradoxically, with the capacity to read in Spanish. I learned the phonetic value of each letter, to decode words. My training included daily out-loud-readings of five pages from Mao Tse-Tung's *Little Red Book*.

As I read, my uncle would correct my pronunciation and intonation. It was impossible for me to understand anything, due to my young age and my basic knowledge of that language. Now you understand why I would lie if I said that I have always loved reading.

Nevertheless, the decoding in and of itself, the mechanical act of reading, became an interesting activity. We would measure the speed I would read a text while clearly articulating each word. I would always read out loud to someone else because for me, at the time, the *raison d'être* of any text was to infuse it with sound. In Mixe, the verb "to talk" is the same as "to read": käjpx, which means "to give voice via your vocal cords". From the beginning, it was clear to me that reading meant, on the one hand, the phonetic articulation of a text and, on the other hand, the understanding of the meaning of its words and their comprehension. Now that I manage both aspects of reading, I realize that I first learned, in spite of everything, to enjoy the pure act of decoding sounds without understanding them. That is the only reason why I still read out loud anytime I have a chance, any text I come across, even if I don't quite understand it: "Water, sodium sulphate, dimethicone, coco-betaine, sodium chloride, glycol distearate" (text on a shampoo bottle).

With time, as I learned how to speak Spanish, these sound constructions started to make sense. Islands of meaning emerged from the texts of the book called *Spanish Readings* that we got at school. Additionally, my Uncle Genaro, following his siblings' recommendations, continued teaching me at home. Once we finished Mao's *Little Red Book*, which took us a long time, he gave me a book that would become one of my most cherished *Lecturas clásicas para niños (Classical Readings for Children)*, which were classics of world literature adapted for children, such as: the Vedas, the *Panchatantra*, *One Thousand and One Nights*, the *Iliad*, the *Odyssey*, creation myths from the far east and the west, a careful selection of Jesus' parables, Japanese traditional stories, among many others. I found its illustrations hauntingly beautiful.

The contradiction also lies in that this selection of *Lecturas*, published in 1924, was part of José Vasconcelos' great literacy project. He was one of the most enthusiastic leaders of the creation of a "bronze race" who had to speak Spanish and read the western literary canon. One of the reasons for which I enjoy speaking Mixe is to make José Vasconcelos roll in his grave, but despite it, I cannot deny the influence that

Lecturas had on me. Once I could understand what I was reading, it made me want to know more about the stories. I didn't want to limit my reading to the obligatory hour-long sessions of reading out loud. Instead, I began reading in anticipation and in silence to discover the twists and turns in those tales.

After that book, I read, always guided by my uncles, novels about Russian heroes from the Second World War, such as *A Story About a Real Man* by Boris Polevoi or accounts by teenage Russian spies in *Por la senda de los valientes: Relatos acerca de jóvenes héroes de la Gran Guerra Patria* (the title in English would be *In the Path of the Brave: Stories of Young Heroes During the Great Patriotic War*). We also combined those readings with an odd combination of texts by Mexican poets such as Amado Nervo, José Manuel Othón, or Sor Juana Inés de la Cruz. Sometime later, we started reading Tolstoy, Pushkin, Chekov, and once we were done with those, Dostoyevsky and Walt Whitman. Most of these books were published by *Editorial Progreso*.

The books arrived one by one and, many times, they also left, which is why the small three-shelf bookcase at home never overflowed. My grandmother taught me to treat books with reverence, as objects of worship on which it was unimaginable to leave any mark. One had to read them with recently washed hands and, preferably, lining its covers with paper or plastic, while we were handling them. My grandfather consulted the dictionary and asked us to do the same. The day that my Uncle Genaro had to migrate, he left me only with one piece of advice. He told me in Mixe "go to the library but read only the books that have the word classic in its covers or in its prologue. If it has that word, it is something you can read". I followed his recommendation, with sadness because of his absence, but with the discipline that was born out of the love I have for him. As a consequence, I didn't know much about contemporary writers until I moved to the city to start high school. I didn't know anything about avant-garde literature, and, except for Amado Nervo and a few other poets, I couldn't stand free verse without measured verses.

Besides reading to my grandmother the letters that she received, she also assigned me a time to read out loud and a time to do my embroidery. If the text was interesting, I would translate it to Mixe. My grandmother would frequently interrupt me to complain or comment on certain passages. For example, she was annoyed when the ungrateful Aeneas abandoned Dido. My mother's name is Eneida and that, in addition to the word "classic" in the book cover, were the criteria to check out the *Aeneid*. We read *The Divine Comedy* together. Years later, I studied literature in college, surprised there was a major for that, and everything changed for me. I'm still pondering whether it did so for the better.

When I was twenty years old, I learned to read and write in Mixe. It's been a fascinating process in which I've joined the efforts that Mixe activists started over thirty years ago, when several of them met to propose the development of a unified alphabet for all variants of our language. It thrills me to collaborate on the creation of reading materials in my mother tongue and on teaching the language, in order for those materials to find readers. I hope that at the end of my life I can have a bookcase full of volumes in Mixe on diverse topics. A bookcase that at least is as big as the one I had in my childhood; medium-sized, not too tall, with three shelves. A bookcase and a community of Mixe-speaking readers with whom to share reactions to the texts.

Despite my current enthusiasm for reading, I would consider it more of an obsession, the circumstances in which a group of children living in the Mixe Sierra learned how to read in the 1980s make me certain that being illiterate cannot be an insult. How could it be when the vast majority of holders of Mixe knowledge don't know how to read or write, either in Mixe or Spanish? I am also certain that reading does not make us better people. There is no way that is a fact. Reading allows us to access a medium in which knowledge is transmitted. Only one among several more, although this is the one politically privileged.

My language is at risk of becoming extinct. Our knowledge, our ritual language, the poetic forms, our oral history are all in danger. The memory of our senior specialists are oral libraries threatened by the fire of forced Hispanization that is now stronger than ever. As I read in Spanish, the Mixe oral tradition is disappearing, the traditional spaces for the transmission of this knowledge have been replaced by schools. It is curious how we lament when someone is illiterate, but no one laments that other types of knowledge, such as oral tradition, is disappearing, especially in Spanish.

Each time that I choose to read a book, it reminds me that it is offered only in a limited number of languages. Each time that I choose a certain type of linguistic exchange, for example, when I choose to have a conversation in Spanish, I am choosing who is my interlocutor. What lies within the fact that a language has printed books are multiple political, historical, economic, and social reasons. It doesn't matter that many of the Mesoamerican languages, such as Mixe, were one of the first to have a written form. Nowadays, from the existing six thousand languages spoken worldwide, only a few have the means or an industry to create printed materials with which to expand reading. Publications, be it in print or electronic, therefore, are immersed in a network knit by colonialism.

Many of the written traditions of Mesoamerican languages were explicitly prohibited and fought against with the establishment of the national state in Mexico. There is nothing aseptic to an act that seems so innocent, so recommendable: reading. Nothing. That is why each time that I take the time to read in Spanish or English, I enjoy it, but I also ponder. I think, and out of that joy comes my anguish. I mostly enjoy reading. But that is not entirely true, sometimes I prefer to listen to Mixe oral tradition.

Industrial Publishing

How to Prepare Yourself for the Collapse of the Industrial Publishing System[1]

Eric Schierloh

Translated by Eric Schierloh and Paul Holzman

> Using Bruce Charles Mollison's *How to Prepare for the Collapse of Capitalism* as a starting point, Eric Schierloh partially rewrites and expands far beyond it. The idea of "agricultural reform" that appears in this anarchist flattening of the hierarchy of urgency was outlined metaphorically, and only a few days apart, by two of the author's friends who don't know each other. For this, he thanks Chilean poet Diego Alfaro Palma and the Argentine letterpress printer stranded in Italy, Federico Cimatti of Prensa La Libertad.

Learn to print, not a text but a book, and not just using a home printer. A typewriter, stamps, engraving, silkscreen printing, letterpress, collage; this can all be useful for writing and for the book outside of the industrial publishing system.

The industrial publishing system implies, to some degree, a standardization of text (edition) and material for the marketplace, in addition to economic dependency—in the vast majority of cases pitiful and meager and altogether unfair in terms of percentages—both symbolically

---

1 Schierloh, Eric, and Paul Holzman. "How to Prepare Yourself for the Collapse of the Industrial Publishing System." *World Literature Today* 95, no. 2 (2021): 16-18. https://dx.doi.org/10.1353/wlt.2021.0137.

and instrumentally. Very few writers know how to make a book, and perhaps even far less want to manufacture them.

The material diversity of the publications will never be industrial because the very nature of the industry is replication, centralization, and an endless increase of revenue to the detriment of everything else. Meanwhile, your nature as a being inserted into a dynamic system (which includes the biblio-system) is, first of all, diversity. So take that diversity to the text as a writer and to the book as a publisher—ultimately, toward a new art of making books.

Allow failure and error to have a place in your procedures.

Publishing outside of the industrial publishing system implies printing, layout, designing, collating, and, in some ways, bookbinding. It is the incessant division of professional work, which then wants to see an overexploitation by oneself. Instead it is a series of possibilities to expand the dimensions of the work. In short, it is about getting involved beyond the text (the more the better), in other instances (the more the better), and with new tools (the more, especially of your ownership, the better) for the production of the book.

Create a similar link with the diverse set of materials of artisan publishing (papers, cardboards, threads, glue, clothes, etc.), with tools and crafts (printing, design, editing and publishing, bookbinding) to that which is created naturally while writing. Where industry fosters or imposes a division (between writing and publishing, text and book, publishing and manufacturing), there it is necessary to restore or (re)build links that give grounds for a productive and political continuity.

Set up a publishing project that transcends self-publication to some degree, in order to shape a community of better interconnected peers and a small, frequently visited community of recognizable individual beings—participants. Join in with the participants and look for ways to dwell in a more complete and committed way in that community. The publishing project is inhabited by artisan publishing, but the community is inhabited, in addition, by the sharing of knowledge, by attending fairs and other kinds of meetings, by discussing and politicizing editing and publishing, and ultimately by collaborating in the most direct and effective way possible with the collapse of the industrial publishing system just as we know it today.

The collapse of the industrial publishing system is due to its replicate nature, its asymmetric business efficiency, its professionalization of all areas in publishing, and to its bureaucratization of both personal and community ventures. The collapse of the industrial publishing system implies the collapse of the culture industry linked to the texts and books produced within the former.

Artisan publishing articulates in the workshop: by the praxis of craft, in the spaces of horizontal socialization, within the community of its peers, and by using multiple tools, disciplines, and types of contacts and possibilities. In the face of growing industrialization and the division and specialization of labor—and even its complete split—appear the workshop, craft, and the community as the space and occasion for increasing self-management.

Where the industrial book ends, the possibility of the artisan book is born. There is a lot to learn from the practice of disposal, especially from the waste of the industrial publishing system. The garbage can in the publisher's workshop can also be revealing. Reusing materials must be a concern for two main reasons: first, it is not one for the industry, and second, it is an ever-growing one for the community of artisan publishers and readers alike.

Develop practical skills beyond writing such as: creative reading, rewriting and appropriation, translation and versioning, printing using various techniques and materials, designing, drawing, photography, publishing as a criterion, bookbinding, reusing materials, the creation of financial mechanisms and distribution strategies, practicing coexistence in a community of peers, etc. In other words, increase writing. Because that is the natural way toward artisan publishing.

Artisan publishing is the publication of texts with the body.

One of the pillars of the industrial publishing system is the private property exerted over the text. Allow digital access, untethered circulation of electronic texts, and take ownership of the book.

Share and teach your skills. And above all, share and teach what you have learned on your own—starting with the context and conditions that made it possible and necessary for you to teach yourself something. And before entering any college to study a craft, pay Jean-Joseph Jacotot a visit.

Join a community of peers where people consume, share, and—when able—produce both individually and collectively (objects, events, situations, ideas, mechanisms, tools, etc.). Artisan publishing is not, of course, exclusively your writing or your artisan publishing house. Artisan publishing is, first and foremost, a collective dynamic that has its own history (long and diverse), which can serve as a brand or guarantee—perhaps much like some parts of the so-called independent publishing community, and as a condition of the deeply biopolitical and micropolitical praxis that deserves to be constantly rethought and updated.

Simplify your writing by freeing it from the paraphernalia of the industrial publishing system. It is necessary to gain space and time in order to increase the dimensions and possibilities of writing, toward printing, editing, bookbinding, and the artisan publishing of books and other textual devices. New meanings, feelings, and encounters await, as well as new possibilities for texts, books, readings, and the publisher's economy.

Discover all that can be done with very little: homemade prints, small unforeseen publications, translations that nobody cares about but will certainly matter to some, the reuse and recovery of scrapped materials, the manufacturing of unique copies in short and slow print runs (book-objects), sketches and prototypes, the exchanging of skills and workforces, the manufacturing of tools (from simple punches and folders to complex machines for engraving, drilling, or even printing), etc.

Also, distance yourself from the logic of unlimited consumption within a culture industry based on incessant rotation and disappearance, excess publication and destruction, propaganda and the promotion of phenomena. Reread, lend, exchange, sell, give away, even reuse these printed materials in your publishing process. If possible, choose artisan publishing products and writings that are made with more care and in a finer way, that have a higher work density, are made by your peers, by small artisan publishing houses or by independent small-industrial publishers that are openly supportive within the biblio-system that we all inhabit.

Exchange output beyond its market value and share the work in its digital format. The cost is almost equal to nothing for both you and the reader. It is also a primary and elementary way of participating in and feeding back into the open-access culture, while giving back a bit of all that we inevitably take from culture.

Spreading the artisan publishing knowledge that is acquired and developed in both an independent and collective fashion is useful for bringing "consumers" to the small-scale production domain. This is central in contributing to the collapse of the industrial publishing system. To put our creative strength, ideas, and symbolic capital in the safekeeping and service of what we seek to weaken is dangerously counterproductive.

Certain laws specific to the industrial publishing system, which work closely with the design of the culture industry, become blurred and lose part of their meaning—if not completely—when culture is distributed and produced with an artisan standard. Such is the case of the paying public domain (a complete contradiction), or of at least certain intellectual property in relation to its materials, length, and scope.

Any recognition at all of an emotional state or condition never has a favorable moment. We are in transition, like a blinking text cursor.

Your creativity—always in relation to the content and processes, to the original and synthetic productions, to the materials and the means of circulation—is the system's limit.

The figures, benefits, and advantages of the industrial publishing system are always relative, misleading, or false. And more often than not, they only reflect the privileged reality of a minority or an elite.

Faced with the incessant proliferation of fashionable texts, the oligopoly of industrialized publishing, and the hyperconcentrated market of global tendency, only the agricultural reform of writing remains. Take this literally. Because collapse conveys a global and complete plummet.

Once a certain point is reached, "there is no possible return." This is the goal to reach.

The Imperfect Edition

Daniel Badenes

Translated by Allison Stickley

> This chapter was originally published as the introduction to Daniel Badenes and Verónica Stedile Luna, eds. *Estado de feria permanente: La experiencia de las editoriales independientes argentinas, 2001-2020* (La Plata: Club Hem Editores, 2020), a collection of studies of independent publishing in Argentina produced by the "La edición en la era de redes" (Publishing in the Era of Networks) project at the Universidad Nacional de Quilmes in La Plata, Argentina. While focused specifically on Argentina, the project's findings about the networked sociability of independent publishers and their defiance of market imperatives are invaluable for understanding the networked practices of independent publishers in many countries of Latin America and beyond. Editorial notes have been added for references to other chapters in Badenes and Stedile's volume or to explain references to Argentine politics and history. The editors thank Badenes, Stedile, and the publishers at Club Hem for allowing us to publish this work in translation.

Focusing on the first two decades of the 21st century, this book[1] looks to explain the political-professional experience, the logical organizational and the aesthetic bets of the "independent publishers", also called "small publishers" or "alternative publishers"—we will already

---

1 Badenes and Stedile, eds. *Estado de feria permanente.*

see the nuances and divergences among these conflicting terms. It constructs a panoramic and polyphonic view of a heterogenous sector that today spans at least 426 active projects [in Argentina], according to a survey we conducted from the Universidad Nacional de Quilmes.[2]

Fully 92.5% of these publishers were born in these twenty years, especially in the five year period between 2011 and 2015, during which four out of every ten currently existing publishers were launched. The neoliberal restoration during Mauricio Macri's presidency reduced but did not stop this phenomenon: one hundred independent labels correspond to those four years of government, that is to say that despite the economic looting and the emptying of cultural policies, projects continued to be developed in Argentina, to the tune of two per month.

At this point, someone could complain, paraphrasing the classic essayist Gabriel Zaid (2001), of *too many publishers*. Instead, I prefer to think about this process as a democratization of publishing work, enabled in part by the technological changes that made editing and designing a book more accessible, and to carry out small print runs with digital printing systems. If not for *too many books*, the resulting books have also been accused more than once for their imperfections, a conservative view that idealized the production of the big-old publishers (as if they have never made a mistake!) and ignore the learning processes and progressive professionalization that runs through the independent sector. In effect, maybe some books published by those publishers—many times one-person projects—have not passed through the same process of correction and editing as an industrial-professional publisher. Even so, we are faced with a notable phenomenon that implies the widening of access to a previously more restricted knowledge and practice, that contribute to pluralism or, said with a word beloved in this time, to bibliodiversity. The *imperfect publisher* is, well, something to celebrate.

I use that adjective in line with the known manifesto written 50 years ago for a reference to the Cuban Revolution. As a director of cinema, Julio García Espinosa assumed he was part of a minority that had been

---

[2] The information corresponds to September 2019 and considers publishers that self-define as independent or are currently named as such in the press or in the call for fairs and related events. The survey is part of the research project "La publicación en la era de redes" ("Publication in the Era of Networks") and the extension project "El Sur tambien publica" ("The South Also Publishes") and has a permanent and dynamic character. The work can be consulted online at lease.web.unq.edu.ar.

able to develop artistic culture by having access to resources which not everybody had within reach. He asked: "What happens if the future is the universalization of education, if economic and social development reduces working hours, if the evolution of cinematographic technique (as there are already obvious signs) makes it possible for it to cease being a privilege of the few(...)?" (What happens, we add here, if the publishing knowledge is within reach of many more?) The Cuban spoke about the possible "act of social justice" and "the true sense of artistic activity" (García Espinosa, 1989: 20). He evoked a phrase from Marx: *In the future there will not be painters but only people who engage in painting among other activities.* And it provokes a question about the meaning of the School of Liberal Arts: Did it make sense to continue developing specialists? The opening of access to means of artistic production—as a process, more so than the results—was the central issue for the *imperfect cinema*, which manifested the cultural commitment of the Cuban Revolution.

The paradox of the current process is that the widening of the publishing field—those *too many publishers*—is negotiated worldwide and locally within the framework of a capitalist system that trends towards increasingly brutal processes of concentration and privatization. Fifteen years ago, in my bachelor's thesis where I investigated the experience of the recovered factories,[3] I noticed this *neoliberal paradox*: "the self-managed practices, when consolidated, contradict the *homo economicus* principles of capitalism, are 'undesired daughters' of this ferocious mode of production. They are the result of the adjustment, privatization, re-regulation, and concentration model (...) The ex-employees of broken, empty, and abandoned factories arrive at cooperativism and self-management out of necessity, not through conviction (...) Self-management is the *backfire* of the neoliberal weapon-project" (Badenes, 2005: 133-134).

---

3   After a massive economic collapse and associated political crisis in Argentina in late 2000-early 2001, workers at enterprises across the country gained recognition as owners of enterprises they had continued to run under collective self-management after their former employers had officially closed them, producing a new category of businesses known as "empresas recuperadas por sus trabajadores" (ERTs, worker-recuperated enterprises). For more in English on this phenomenon, see Marcelo Vieta *Workers' Self-Management in Argentina: Contesting Neo-Liberalism by Occupying Companies, Creating Cooperatives, and Recuperating Autogestión* (Boston: Brill, 2020); on the specific, prominent case of the B.A.U.E.N. Hotel in central Buenos Aires, see Katherine Sobering *The People's Hotel: Working for Justice in Argentina* (Durham: Duke University Press, 2022).

Perhaps the phenomenon of the independent publisher does not have the radicalness of that contradiction—old Taylorist workers tossed into the street constructing a new world—but it goes equally in the face of concentrated capitalism's logic. In one of the pioneering works noting the concentration and foreignization of the Argentine publishing sector in the '90s, Malena Botto points out well: "in front of the transnational conglomerates, small-scale ventures persist or emerge, whose cultural politics exhibit notorious differences in respect to the large groups. We are referring to the traditionally named 'independent presses/publishers', like others that start to appear in the decade of the 1990s and that proliferate in the following decade, the 'small presses/publishers'" (Botto, 2014: 219-220).

Concerning the terminological tension, Hernán Vanoli and Ezequiel Saferstein signal that the category *independent* took on "particular energy starting from 2001, under the form of micropress undertakings that form a heterogenous space" (Vanoli and Saferstein, 2011: 69). This does not mean that they did not exist before: some of these imprints we are referring to were born in the nineties or before, even back in the seventies, but recently they have started to refer to themselves as "independent." Before they were just presses. In the context of concentration and income of foreign capital, the notion of independent presses constructed a figure opposed to the one represented by the transnational publishing groups. This clash where the original definition of independent press lives expresses not just a question of economic ownership but also of project: faced with financial logics, management oriented to high profitability, and *best-sellerization*, independence lives in the "sustained and silent creation of a catalog," together with the commitment to and bet on discovery (Colleu 198, 126).

The Argentine Publishing Structure

> To understand the publishing field not as a unified space but as a space made of many distinct sub-fields that tend to develop their own dynamics, and that see contradictory logics clash within them undoubtedly offers a more exact image of the publishing reality. Consequently, it would be more correct to speak, according to John Thompson, of publishing fields in plural. (Noël, 2018: 26)

This compilation does not analyze the full ensemble of the Argentine publishing system, but one of its actors: the *independent presses*, to use the most frequent denomination. To understand the place that these occupy, it is worth making a parenthesis and to characterize who forms the complete scene. As a reference, the typology of publishers which Carlos Gazzera proposes in his book *Editar: un oficio* (*Publishing: A Profession*) can help us. There, the editor of EDUVIM distinguishes:

- The *publishing groups*, defined as "conglomerates of publishing labels" in which "the search for maximum profitability of everything which is published is not a mere economic principle of organization, it is also a catalog model" (Gazzera, 2016: 55). These groups are the product of a *horizontal integration* that reaches the highest quantity of authors and titles possible by means of the accumulation of imprints and catalogs. Within this category are the groups of national-regional scale (that sometimes maintain dominant positions in some niches of the market), and above all, transnational.

- The *independent publishers*. Although recognized as an ambiguous expression, Gazzera also uses this distinction. His definition first refers to the "imprints that do not have ties with (are independent from) the foreign or Transnational Publishing Groups." From his perspective, that excludes just as many imprints absorbed by the groups as "those publishing houses that have developed processes of internationalization with assets in other countries" (60-61). For Gazzera, therefore, it is "valid to understand the concept of 'independent' as an ideological definition and not structural'" (61).

Such a definition stands out with greater precision upon considering the following types of publishers, which are not connected to the big groups and nevertheless constitute distinct sets from the independents:

- The *vanity publisher* and the process of *self-publishing* that are publication options, but they do not have a catalog policy. Rather, they assume the suppression of the most genuine work of an imprint: to publish (62).

- The *university presses*, defined as those which depend on or have a direct property relation with a public or private university.

- The *State presses*, which is to say those financed by the public budget (excluding, if we take into account the previous type, those of state universities). The paradigmatic example is Mexican: the Fondo de Cultura Económica. We should also mention Monte Ávila in Venezuela. Argentina does not have an experience of this magnitude, although there do exist provincial imprints (like the Fondo Editorial Rionegrino) and municipal (a standout among them is EMR in Rosario), and during isolated periods had some interesting publications from areas like the National Library.

Gazzera considers that independent publishers as well as the university and state ones support pluralism by constructing an "anti-hegemonic catalog" when faced with what is "dictated by marketing."

In this typology, very useful for characterizing the publishing system, what is striking is the absence of the *national publisher*, of the medium-sized company in the market that seems to be in extinction—or is absorbed by the figure of the *independents*, although they do not use that term to define themselves.[4]

A heterogeneous and contested sector

What then are independent publishers? We saw before that this category took on dynamism from the turn of the century. José de Souza Muniz Júnior, who wondered about *independent publishers* as a discursive formula, takes us further back and talks about a preeminence from the mid to late nineties:

> Such representation occupies spaces in the specialized press, in the daily and institutional discourse of the publishers identified with this sign, in the theoretical and semi-theoretical materials produced by some of those publishers (especially in the central countries) and in the instances of action and collective representation that have been created since the end of the '90s. Also, the academic field presents certain unanswered questions about the practices, obligations

---

[4] It is an interesting phenomenon because for a long time the business entities of the sector, the Cámara Argentina del Libro (CAL, the Argentine Chamber of Books) and the Cámara Argentina de Publicaciones (CAP, the Argentine Chamber of Publications) were defined based on a dichotomy that imagined one nucleus of national publishers and another of transnationals, respectively. Strictly speaking, the picture is more complex. First, because no nucleus is exclusively publishers; among their patrons are also bookstores: Cúspide in the case of CAP and a wide range of stores of books in the CAL, that furthermore include graphic companies, a paper mill and other varieties surrounding but that are not part of the publishing sector. Second, the entity of the "nationals" also includes foreign labels like Alianza, Akal, Celtia (Gedisa), Amorrortu, Libros del Zorro Rojo or McGraw Hill. And to characterize the register of 532 partners found in their network is difficult: there are vanity publishers (like Dunken or Tahiel), university publishers, and also two groups with very specific profiles that could widen our typology: the technical and professional (which publish books for attorneys, doctors, etc.) and the religious. These last two make up more than 50 of their members. At the same time, everything outside the Chambers must be thought of: without looking much further than the survey of 426 independent publishers mentioned before, only 17.8% (76) are affiliated with the CAL.

and development of the projects identified, endogenously or exogenously, with this terminology. (de Souza Muniz Jr, 2015: 145)

In 1998 the publishers Lom in Chile, Trilce in Uruguay, Era in Mexico and Txalaparta from the Basque Country formed a group called, early on, *Independent Publishers*. From that space they convened a First Meeting of Independent Publishers in Latin America (Primer Encuentro de Editores Independiente de América Latina), which materialized in May 2000 at the III Salón del Libro Iberoamericano de Gijón (Spain).[5] Adriana Astutti and Sandra Contreras's text (2001), habitually cited among the first works on the topic, gathers the intervention of these publishers—that Beatriz Viterbo had founded in Rosario around 1990—from that encounter which was also attended by the founding publishers of the space along with Cuarto Propio from Chile, Editions la Découverte from France, Vozes from Brazil, and The New Press from the United States the imprint of André Schiffrin, who a year before had published *La edición sin editores* (2000). Colleu (2008: 31) attributes the invention of the term *bibliodiveristy* to the participants of that meeting, a term which will take on force in the following years, especially when it was coupled with a series of actions driven by UNESCO.[6]

Meetings and organizations with this imprint[7] were a show of how, on different points of the globe with distinct publishing traditions, the figure of the *independent publisher* emerges as a self-identification and as a journalistic or academic characterization of a phenomenon. The principle shared characteristic among the countries was the process of concentration and trans-nationalization. But they would have

---

[5] The topic was also present at the International Book Fair in Buenos Aires (May 2001) at a table organized by the Secretary of Culture of the Nation and the Goethe Institute, with the participation of medium scale labels.

[6] I am referring to the Universal Declaration of Cultural Diversity in 2002, and the Convention on the Protection and Promotion of the Diversity of Cultural Expression, adopted in Paris in October 2005.

[7] The succession of milestones in the five years since the First Meeting held in Gijón was notorious. It is worth mentioning the series of institutions created during that period: Asociación de Editores Independientes, Universitarios y Autónomos de Chile—known as Editores de Chile—(2000/2001), the Federazione Italiana degli Editori Independent (2001), LIBRE, in Brazil (2001/2002), the Alianza Internacional de Editores Independientes (2002) who launched their Declaración de Dakar (2003) driven by sixty publishers in forty countries; the Asociación francesa L'Autre Livre (2003), the Alianza de Editoriales Mexicanas Independientes (2004), the Independent Alliance in Great Britain and the Alianza de Editores Independientes de Argentina por la Bibliodiversidad (2005). The list of organizations and associations continues. As de Souza Muniz Jr. signaled, "although they have their particularities (scales of work, level of institutionalization, strategies, etc.), they have as a background the need to give visibility to the production of 'independent' publishers and to fight collectively for their economic and symbolic survival."

been hard pressed to have a single conclusive definition for the "pole" of independent publishers, which a very heterogeneous group expressed in each place: "the idea of bringing them together at a common pole seems hasty," Hernán Vanoli, at that time with the Editorial Tamarisco, considered a decade ago (Vanoli, 2009: 170).

In the same vein, Szpilbarg and Saferstein wrote in 2012: "...although we believe a separation is necessary between these publishers and those that depend on the large concentrated groups, we maintain that the term 'independent' to define them is misleading since we consider there is a marked heterogeneity within this group in terms of their modes of operation, their representation, and their aspirations" (Szpilbarg and Saferstein, 2012: 465).

In another text, when insisting on the "highly heterogeneous" composition of the sector of independent publishers that publish literature, Vanoli affirms that it includes: (1) small and medium businesses; 2) *amateur* publishers of *intervention*[8] with industrial production, and 3) artisanal publishers (Vanoli, 2010: 135).

Further on, Vanoli offers another classification, where the second and third types stay in the same group.[9] While the first *businesses* would be the ones represented by the Alianza Internacional de Editores[10] on a worldwide level, there is "a wide range of informal, precarious publishers outside statistics, nourished by self-employment, who bet

---

8 The two words in italics come verbatim from Vanoli's article. The problems of a definition based on ameturism should be noted, as Sophie Noël does in La edición independiente crítica: "The border between professional publishing and amateur publishing," she writes, "is extremely unstable and evolutionary, something characteristic of artistic fields. Creating a strict separation between two categories does not seem pertinent among the cases of structures for which professionalization constitutes an essential question" (Noël, 2018: 50). For this author, the independent experiences reactivate a tension between the vocational mode and the professional mode, but they blur the boundaries between amateur publishing and professional publishing" (142).

9 In the perspective of this book [Estado de feria permanente] we prefer to support the triad. There are at least 36 active artisan publishers, who define themselves as such and whose projects have characteristic features, some of which are analyzed by Joaquín Conde and Lea Hafter in chapter 8 [of Estado de feria permanente], where they elaborate an idea of art-publication. Some analysts—such as Ana Mazzoni and Damián Selci—link artisanal publishing to a boom in design as a discipline that began in the mid-1990s.

10 At that time, a "collective of independent publishers for bibliographic diversity from Argentina" had also been formed at the local level, later called the "Alianza Editores Independientes Argentinos por la Bibliodiversidad," which used the acronym EDINAR. Promoted since 2005, its main activity took place around 2010 and 2011. Some thirty small and medium-sized publishers participated in the space, including La marca and Interzona, el 8vo loco, Lenguaje Claro, Prometeo, and Colihue.

on militancy in literary culture with subsistence economies" (Vanoli, 2010: 143).[11]

Among these latter publishers, it is common to identify as "self-managing" or "alternative,"[12] with an imprint that spreads from social organizations (Botto, 2012: 227). For several years, the principal reference for them was the countercultural space known as the *FLIA*, an acronym for *Feria del Libro Independiente* that leaves the significance of the A in suspense, which is not *Argentina* but rather *autónoma* (autonomous), *amiga* (friendly), *alternativa* (alternative), *autogestiva* (self-managed), *amorosa* (loving), *andariega* (restless), *alocada* (hectic), *abierta* (open), *antipatriarcal* (antipatriarchial). Oriana Seccia defines it as "a festival where independent publishers and individuals present their books and fanzines, designers offer their products, and where they hold live musical performances, readings, and political declamations (generally of denouncement)" (Seccia, 2012: 81-82).[13]

The first FLIA was held in 2006, though Winik (2010) recognizes its origins in an assembly of independent writers formed in 2001, Szpilbarg (2015) signals another possible precursor in *)el asunto(*[14], and Saferstein (2012: 183) dates it even further back to the "Counterfair" held by a group of poets from the literary circle "*Maldita Ginebra*" outside of

---

11 The idea of production that escapes the statistics is not strictly speaking local. It also appears in Noël's book—which studies French independent publishing—for whom these imprints form "a kind of ´underground economy´" (Noël, 2018: 49).

12 In his latest book, almost a decade after the article that we return to here, Vanoli expresses his preference for the term alternative publishers: "The production logics of the counterculture—generation of alternative circuits to the concentrated market, promotion of values that do not celebrate mainstream consumption, urban bohemian lifestyle combined with social democratic consensus—are far from being 'independent', since their identity is based on the dependence on a multiplicity of factors, among which the economic one is not the least important" (Vanoli, 2019: 95). He also points out that several alternative publishers "operate as a side business for millionaires," based on family fortunes (102). Thus, it ends up in expressions such as "poor alternative publishers" or "militant alternative publishers," as opposed to those that have "financial and commercial backing," and that also tend to integrate vertically (117).

13 Anyone (rather, anyone who identifies as self-managed and independent) can participate in the FLIA, which has meant that in many of its local editions and expressions, book stalls coexist on an equal footing—and even in the background—with others dedicated to textiles, food, crafts, and movies.

14 Also mentioned by Matías Reck in chapter 6 of this book [*Estado de feria permanente*]. Founded and coordinated by Pablo Strucchi in 2001,)el asunto("appeared as a space for publishing and disseminating books without establishing itself as a classic publishing house with a catalog. This project also sought to speed up the path for authors who wanted to publish their books, as well as facilitating the distribution of books from the meeting between the author and the reader without going through the distributor and the space of the bookstore" (Szpilbarg, 2015b).

the FILBA. In the case of the FLIA, although the first edition did in fact have the label, it soon stopped being defined as a counterfair; what characterizes it is not a subversion of the mainstream field but its intent to create an alternative field (Saferstein, 2012).

Perhaps *amateur* is no longer the most adequate word to use, but the idea of *militancy* is. Like the community media and the cultural centers to which they are tied, they think beyond profitability. It could be said they are not for profit, which does not mean they are for loss, but that they ignore the economic side of their practices, as will be seen in the following chapter.

In short—and in sum—we can talk about more than 400 independent publishers if we construct that group from the heterogeneity that goes from the small business publisher to the militant collectives that *intervene* by publishing, and from the industrial imprints to the artisanal projects whose publishers make their books with their own hands and defend minimal print runs. Within this large group, diverse opinions can be found about the rights of the author and copyright licenses, links with the State, decisions of where to print and why, and relationships with the booksellers, among other issues. At times more defined and characterizable subgroups emerge that test proper names,[15] although when it comes to the fairs, we again find them under the umbrella of "independent publishers." In the end, it is the expression with the most history, that managed to convert itself into a brand, and, as Eric Schierloh says (2019), has an aura to it.

Something similar happens with research about the topic. We can—we will continue doing so in the following pages—test definitions and refine indicators that carefully carve out our aim: there will always be an exception that we want to include. That's how we spent two years with *Editar sin patrón* (*Publishing Without a Mold/Publishing Without a Boss*)[16] a book about the *independent* production of magazines that we only think about as a precursor to this compilation. There we wrote:

---

[15] A very obvious case is the artisan or home edition, "a sub-area with its own history and relative autonomy, and which, although it is also under development, has an increasing presence and representation in the various circuits, both official and alternative or peripheral" (Schierloh, 2019).

[16] The word "patrón" can be used to mean both a pattern or mold one follows to make an object (cross-stitch pattern, for example) or to mean one's boss at work. Both senses work in the case of this title.

> It is difficult to find a unique and exhaustive formulation that covers each of the titles in the sum of the texts referred to that make up this book. One could have tried, and then excluded every reference that didn't fit. However, it was intentional to instead include them all, rather than giving in to a classificatory rigor that would have given the researcher peace of mind but taken away from the dynamism and diversity of the aim that calls to us. (Badenes, 2017: 20)

The term *independent* is imperfect, flexible and will always be "plagued by exceptions and contradictions," as López Winne and Malumián say.[17] In each investigation, in each debate, in each manifesto appear frequent searches of other terms, other definitions or at least challenges to the original term, in which they in turn interact.

Ten years ago, in an article published by Sonia Budassi in *Perfil* (often cited in later works about the topic), the editor of Gog y Magog, Miguel Petrecca, it is defined as: "we are the contrary: we are an extremely dependent publisher, dependent on the value of the peso, the price of paper, the politics of subsidies, or rather, much more dependent than a big publisher" (Budassi, 2018). In the French investigation that we have already cited, an interviewee—defined as "in a voluntary servitude"—questions the term in the same sense: "we depend on subsidies, on distributors, on bookstores, on the ideology, on the idiocy of the time, on everything" (Noël, 2018: 52). The reference brings to mind the slogan of the magazine *El Molino de Pimienta*, born in the first years of the '80s, that was defined as a "dependent magazine" and explained in its *Introduction Letter*: "… it will be a dependent publication (…) it will depend, among other things, on the generosity of friends, on the mood of the printer, on the literacy level of the curator.…"

For his part, in his thesis and later book about poetry publishers in the '90s, Matías Moscardi—defining a way of writing and a way of making these projects—opts to talk about *"interdependent* publishers," an expression that has a specific meaning but at the same time functions in intertextually with the *native term*.

---

[17] These authors suggest "thinking of the independent as a zone within the field of publishing. An area in constant tension where there are various actors fighting to appropriate it and speak on its behalf. It is a political area, unstable and constantly changing. Thinking of the independent as a zone instead of a category allows us to abandon the binary that the category implies (…) There are publishers that at a given moment in their evolution may be within this zone of the field and in their future move away" (López Winne and Malumian, 2016: 2).

> Interdependent publishers would be, as a first definition, projects that present an inseparable link between text and materiality, genre and format, aesthetics and modes of circulation, but also work in a strongly relational way, not only in terms of their forms of cooperative management but also in regards to the writings and poetics that we find in their catalogs. The figure of interdependent publishers allows us to think of series, constellations, blocks, machines, apparatuses, that is, devices for collective enunciation or relational forms of writing and publishing. (Moscardi, 2016: 22)

As a general rule, there doesn't seem to be an alternative term to stand in for and construct the group of independent publishers, self-identified as such or the hetero-identification on the part of certain actors in the publishing field (for example, book fair organizers), or from the journalistic and academic sphere.

Once this limitation is assumed, I believe that three great ideas are able to be recognized around which the definition of *independent publisher* revolves in those identifications: one referring to property and organizational forms, another linked to the catalogs, and finally a third that puts focus on the *sociability* of the publishers and the formation of reading communities.

Independence as antagonist to economic concentration

As Noël (2018) advises, part of the controversy over the notion of independence is its relative character: it is independent with respect to something or someone. So the idea "has seen its definition evolve with the passing of time" and, after being "largely brandished against political power, today is principally opposed to the economic and financial forces embodied by large groups, and constitutes an important focus of fights in the heart of cultural spaces" (Noël, 2018: 51-52).

In the Meeting of Independent Publishers in 2000,[18] Pablo Harari (director of Editorial Trilce, founded in 1985) defined the *independent publisher*

> in opposition to publishers which are part of conglomerates or groups (most often multinationals). These group together many

---

[18] The acts in their entirety are available at https://www.oei.es/historico/cultura2/actas.htm

publishing labels and generally various industry sectors (publishing, bookstores, printing, advertising); and/or are multimedia (books, press, audiovisual, music, Internet), etc. (Harari, 2000)

Just as we saw with Gazzera, keeping in mind that university publishers, for example, could be encompassed in this definition, he added: "Although they have many elements in common, I also do not include among the independent publishers those that depend financially and hierarchically on the State or institutions."

As previously mentioned, this is the first and principal definition of the notion of *independent publisher*. In an article published the following year in *Revista Iberoamericana*, Astutti and Contreras reported "a widespread consensus in the interventions (written and oral) of the participants" that defined the *independent* publisher "in relation to the conglomerates, almost always of transnational character." It is, fundamentally, an "independence against the imperative of maximum profitability," which is linked to "the priority given to the quality and cultural value of the book (above its other aspects of economic good and product of the cultural industry)" (Astutti and Contreras, 2001: 768).[19] Also linked to the idea of national independence (in the case of Schiffrin), this condition proposes them as guarantees of diversity and pluralism, principles threatened by economic concentration.

The *independent edition* then constitutes a replica of the process—accelerated in the '90s—of purchasing and concentration of national publishers on the part of foreign conglomerates, which introduced global editing forms and financial logics, and broke the *traditional family business* (Botto, 2006; Szpilbarg and Saferstein, 2012; De Diego, 2012).

At the same time, as Verónica Stedile Luna (2017) observed, in the case of magazines, a curious semantic displacement adds other meanings to the word *independent,* which is linked to the horizontality of the

---

19 For the publishers in Rosario, however, that definition was not sufficient. It became necessary "to problematize the, in immediate appearance, the equation independent publisher = a good publisher / transnational publisher = poor quality; for another, to warn that the opposition independent / multinational is not sufficient to explain the entire field, that within the independent publishers, we must also distinguish the, let us say, 'small' publishers, whose proliferation, at least since the 1990s in Argentina, constitutes a unique cultural phenomenon." (768) In relation to this last point, what they tried was to make a distinction of scale, it could be said, among "large independent publishers" like Anagrama or Pre-textos, and other experiences such as that of Beatriz Viterbo herself or Adriana Hidalgo, Simurg, Paradiso, Tierra Firme, Alción, Siesta, Zapatos Rojos, Tse-Tse, Vox, Melusina and El Broche.

work or the plebeian origin of economic resources. In other words, at least in the subgroup of the underground, militant or political-cultural publishers, "independent" would also mean "self-managed" and name an organizational form without bosses[20] which as Pablo González signals in chapter 3,[21] sometimes is confused with *entrepreneurship* and becomes self-exploitation.

Independence as a catalog project

Outside the economic-organizational terrain, another idea independent publishers put into play at the time of defining themselves is the project: the idea of a coherent cultural position around certain themes that hatch the publication of *long sellers* and aspires to generate a publishing collection. This is what is usually implicit in the notion of a catalog.

The centrality of the catalog is a rule that prevails in *Independientes ¿de qué? (Independent of What?)*, published by the editors of Godot in a collection from the Fondo de Cultura Económica (López Winne and Malumián, 2016). There the authors signal the relation to the market as the primary issue: "an independent publisher must think about their catalog as bound to the coherence of its content and not to the thematic trends that run through the publishing market. It must, in every moment, support a catalog as a collection" (López Winne and Malumián, 2016: 5). Of course, this doesn't imply inattention to the economic dimension.[22] But the key to recognizing an independent publisher would be in the catalog, the design, the quality of production... In this sense, Colleu proposes—in line with the Alianza de Editores Independientes—to use the term *creative independent publisher* (Colleu, 2008: 27, 121).

---

20 Nonetheless, it is interesting to note that this self-management stamp rarely translates into legal forms. Even when it seems logical to find—in a sector where the self-management discourse prevails—work cooperatives, this legal translation of the experiences is unusual. Barely twelve of the 426 publishers surveyed (less than 3%) are defined as cooperatives. Several of them come from the graphic sector and formed the cooperative before turning to editorial work, like El Zócalo (CABA), Veintinueve de mayo (Córdoba), or Sietesellos (Santa Rosa). Founded in 1973, Patria Grande is a kind of pioneer in the cooperative publishing field.

21 Referring to Pablo Amadeo González "Relatos sobre trabajo en pequeñas editoriales" in Badenes and Stedile, eds. *Estado de feria permanente*, 63-84.

22 "The course of its catalog has to be marked by quality but without neglecting returns" (López Winne and Malumián, 2016: 4). For the authors, disinterest in economic health should not be understood as a gesture of independence (9).

> Creative independent creative publishers seek coherence in their catalog; over the years they weave the fabric of their legitimacy by producing books that resonate together. They are alternately discoverers, research laboratories, committed political actors. (126)

We return to *Independientes ¿de qué?*: only after the catalog does the matter of ownership and capital contribution appear, in a definition by refusal: "An independent publisher is not able to be part of an economic group, nor take its editorial decisions based on pressure from shareholders" (López Winne and Malumián, 2016: 9).[23] However, when outlining the contradictions in the term, they mention Constantino Bértolo's position, "who founded a kind of independent press—Caballo de Troya—within a publishing conglomerate—Random House" (2). In short, for these authors, an independent publisher

> is one that has its North focused on the construction of a quality catalog but without neglecting to look at the project's profitability. It pursues self-sustainability and does not depend on any capital contribution that comes from outside its editorial activity. (...) [T]he dissemination of what is published or rejected is completely under the command of its editor (López Winne and Malumián, 2016: 14)

Thus appears the question of bibliodiversity, which is "the value the independent publisher brings" (López Winne and Malumián, 2016: 6). Noël identifies it as one of the principle argumentative lines in defense of the independent publisher—"less radical and apocalyptic" than the complaint about homogenization (2018: 122), although he notes the risk of falling into "quantitative" definitions in which publishers "fail to oppose more than the vague notion of 'diversity for quality.'" The defense of diversity as an end "continues being one of the most mobilized topics at this pole of the publishing field and the difficulty for publishers consists in defending a qualitative conception of the concept" (Noël, 2018: 124).

The idea of bibliodiversity began to take off in 2005. That year, in the setting of the Latin world's leading book fair, the conference

---

[23] The definition falls in line by the one laid out by Colleu (2008: 96): "the publisher's power of decision must be total: whatever the legal structure chosen, no external 'shareholder' must be able to prevent it." Therefore, the French writer adds, "it is essential that no one financially associated in the capital of the company, the banks, pension funds, insurance, etc., have profit objectives that are incompatible with the editorial policy of creating" (96).

"Independent publishers of the Latin world and bibliodiversity" was held, organized by the Guadalajara International Book Fair, the Alianza de Editores Independientes (born three years before), the Unión Latina and CERCALC.[24] From there arose a declaration signed by some 70 independent publishers from 23 countries, very in line with the cultural diversity proposals promoted by UNESCO.

During those same years, Gilles Colleu published La edición independente como herramienta protagónica de la bibliodiversidad (Independent Publishing as a Leading Tool for Bibliodiversity, 2006 in France; the Argentine edition from 2008 is by La Marca Editora, whose editor Guido Indij got EDINAR going). He was one of the participants at the Guadalajara meeting, and we have already cited him in reference to the idea of "editors of creation." For Colleu the creative book was the incarnation of bibliodiversity, for its opposition to the phenomena of best-sellerization (Colleu, 2008: 30-31).

> Faced with financial logics, more and more independent publishers are reacting, multiplying resistance strategies and contributing to the maintenance of a plural, committed, exciting publishing capable of offering readers the thousand flavors of the world, the infinity of peoples' ideas, the diversity of cultures, instead of the lukewarm soup possessed by some groups of industrial publishers' in the world. (25)[25]

Note how, according to José de Souza Muniz Júnior, the independent publisher configures one "ethical category" that represents a "pole of resistance": "The idea of an 'independent' publisher is forged as one that, remaining outside of these large groups, maintains total autonomy over the formation of its catalog and privileges quality to the detriment of profitability" (de Souza Muniz Jr, 2015: 146).

---

24 Although it was held in Mexico, the meeting had a predominantly European participation (fourteen publishers in total, compared to nine American and two African). There were no Argentinian participants. In the resulting document, contributions can be found from the following: Éditions Métaillié, L´Atelier, Chandeigne, Vents d´ailleurs, Éditions Actes Sud (France), Tusquets, Anagrama, Castille (Spain), Voland, Nottetempo (Italy), Éditions d´en bas (Suiza), Humanitas (Romania), Chá de Caxine (Angola), Presses Universitaires d´Afrique (Cameroon), Éscrits des Forges, L´instante même (Quebec), Ediciones Sin Nombre, Colibrí, El Tucán de Virginia, Ediciones del Ermitaño (Mexico), LOM (Chile), Trilce (Uruguay), Libre (Brazil).

25 Colleu clarifies that he does not criticize "the commercial aspect of book publishing" but rather "the financial drift of this commercialization," the process of financialization of book publishing, by which "books are published like yogurts are produced" (29, 25-26).

In July 2007, reunited in Paris, the same group of publishers made a new declaration (the third after Dakar and Guadalajara) "for the protection and promotion of bibliodiversity." There they suggested:

> The role of independent publishers as essential actors in the dissemination of ideas, in the construction of human beings, is seriously threatened throughout today's world. Bibliodiversity—cultural diversity in relation to the book—is in danger.

Independent publishers are suffering intensely from the effects of economic globalization, which favors financial concentration in the sector, dominated today by large groups that own economic resources, the media, and dissemination mechanisms. The standardization of content is underway.

Purely financial logic pushes the publishing world toward a commodification incompatible with the creation and dissemination of cultural goods. Despite that, the book should be a public good (cited in Colleu, 2008: 203).

Thus, the notion of independent publications stayed intrinsically associated with the new *biodiversity* formula. In the following decade, the Alianza Internacional de Editores Independientes titled their magazine as such (*Bibliodiversity*, which published six issues since 2011), and like Colleu a decade before, the Australian inspiration Susan Hawthorne published a new manifesto.[26] Revisiting the analogy with biodiversity, it is clear that *bibliodiversity* is not simply *many books*: It is also preserving the "equilibrium between species" (that no species/publisher that can extinguish another) and to guarantee a publishing life in accordance with local conditions. "Those of us who produce or cultivate bibliodiversity live socially, politically, sometimes geographically and linguistically, in the margins," Hawthorne summarizes (2018: 43) in line with a qualitative definition of the values being defended.

---

26 Three aspects that stand out in Hawthorne's gaze: her Australian nationality, environmental concern, and feminist militancy. The first implies the use of a peripheral English with its own identity: it helps to think that there are no "unique" or "neutral" versions of a language (in the same way that publishers in our region defend Argentine translations against standard Spanish). The second introduces the concern for an organic, conscious, sustainable publishing industry. The third is the most interesting vein in her book. It brings history to the relationship between publishing and feminism: faced with a phenomenon that one imagines is recent, Hawthorne refers, for example, to an International Feminist Book Fair held in 1984, which brought together editors and writers from different continents.

The local character of experiences is not a minor issue. It constitutes another point of confrontation with the Economic Groups—the transnational and also the national—what great commercial-industrial publisher operates outside of a national capital? As Eliana Tessio Conca observes in her thesis, "business concentration...is not only economic, but also geographical" (Tessio Conca, 2017: 38). In the case of independent publishers, although 69% are concentrated in the city and province of Buenos Aires (where half of the population lives) it is possible to identify 132 experiences in the so-called "interior" of the country: 22.1% in the central zone, 4.2% in the northwest, 2.6% in Patagonia, 1.4% in Cuyo, and 0.7% in the northeast.[27] And fortunately there are more and more initiatives to know and analyze them, compared to the initial moment when academia was very focused on the experience of Buenos Aires.[28]

That also implies thinking about other spaces for meeting and circulation. Thus, although many works that reflect on the sector's fairs usually stopped in the FLIA and in the Feria de Editores (FED), as Ezequiel Saferstein and Víctor Malumián do very well in this compilation,[29] others must also be taken into account, like La Bastardilla in Córdoba, Fluye in Paraná and Santa Fe, the FER in Rosario, FEA Bahía Blanca or the Feria Temporalmente Autónoma (FTA) in Neuquén, in addition to some provincial festivals—promoted by local publishers and poets—within which other fairs have grown.[30] With these references derived from the territorial dimension of bibiliodiversity, we enter into the third dimension that could define the independent publishers: the permanent fair state.[31]

---

27 According to the survey carried out by our research project, already cited.

28 Tessio Conca analyzes experiences from Entre Ríos. Lucía Coppari studies the sociability of small presses in Córdoba. Ignacio Ratier studies the independent publishing space in Santiago del Estero.

29 Referring to Ezequiel Saferstein "Las ferias de libros y sus públicos" in Badenes and Stedile, eds. *Estado de feria permanente*, 241-254, and Víctor Malumián "La feria como diálogo entre editores y lectores" in ibid., 255-264.

30 Two notorious cases are the Festival Internacional de Poesía de Rosario (FIPR) and the Festival Internacional de Literatura de Tucumán (FILT). At the same time, as Vanoli signals in his last book, obligatory cultural programming makes it so that "book fairs more and more resemble festivals," just like what happens with the Festival Internacional de Literatura de Buenos Aires (FILBA) organized by Eterna Cadencia (Vanoli, 2019: 147). In both movements, the distinction between fair and festivals is blurred, and to define a book fair/festival/party becomes as difficult as finding the definition of independent publisher.

31 This is a literal translation of Badenes and Stedile's book's title (Estado de feria permanente), which is itself a pun on the phrase "estado de sitio permanente" ("permanent state of siege"), a phrase commonly used by dictatorial states in Latin America to describe and justify the suspension of legal and civil rights as a state of permanent exception from the rule of law.

Sociability and militancy of independent publishing

One of the characteristics of these publishers—signaled by Vanoli (2009) and well covered in chapter 13 of this book[32]—is that they orient their production to a specific reading community, rather than to the indifferent public. In this sense, the editor of Crisis and ex Tamarisco maintain that, much more than their *independence* from transnational capital or their condition as "niche publishers," what characterizes independent publishers "is the use of creativity as input for generating reading communities" (Vanoli, 2009: 172).

> Rather than oriented exclusively to a market of anonymous readers, the small publishers that interest us, largely born in the period after 2001 (Carne Argentina, Mansalva, Clase Turista, Entropía, El Andariego, Editorial Funesiana, La Creciente, Eloísa Cartonera, among others) aspire to function in many cases as organizing principles for reading communities where face-to-face meetings, the system of virtual sociability built around various spaces of registration such as weblogs and personal pages, and mostly events, book presentations, live readings, and fairs constitute a repertoire of initiatives that, in many cases strengthened by the self-management ideals that different Argentine cultural formations carried out as resistance after the economic-political-institutional debacle of the beginning of the century, appear as a common horizon that functions as the cement of the various forms of what we could call literary militancy. (173)

In this relational aspect we can find another approach to the imperfect definition of the independent publisher: the sociability of the sector that puts into play an affective dimension, defines a form of militancy, and places the link with readers in a fundamental position.

The focus is now not only on "bibliophilia" and the love for literature that mobilizes publishers but also on the "bonus of sociability and activism that transcends the invoice of books as objects, with a very different repertoire of action" (175). This "new form of cultural activism," according to Vanoli, "uses different strategies for generating social relationships and collaborative networks within literary culture" (176).

---

[32] Paula Cuestas and Rodolfo Iuliano "Las editoriales independientes y sus lectores imaginados" in Badenes and Stedile, eds. *Estado de feria permanente*, 219-232.

From this perspective, the key element that defines the independent publisher is creativity, which is expressed in different ways: in the design (which Carolina Muzi analyzes interestingly in chapter 11 of this book),[33] in the construction of the book as a material object, in the work of diffusion in the virtual world, and finally in the organization of distinct activities "where reading communities structured around this circuit of small publishers are updated in face-to-face interaction" (179).

In a festive climate, no doubt a tributary of the rock music world that functioned as an important countercultural resistance in the years of the military dictatorship,[34] "supporting" [hacer el aguante] the narrative in these events certainly implies participating in a register of emerging practices where sociability is more similar to that of a small band's concert than to the gatherings or conferences typical of literary modernity (179).

Among the activities that make up this web of sociability, Vanoli points out in his text "the organization and participation of publishers at events, readings, fairs and other instances." The third part of this collection contributes precisely to thinking about those areas: most of all the fair, but also the festivals and reading series that Cristian Molina characterizes very well from the experience of Ediciones Arroyo in the outskirts of Santa Fe.

It could be said that with these practices, with the formation of reading communities with an in-person and interactive character, the publishers effectively constitute a nucleus of resistance to the entertainment industry. This is how we return, it seems, to the original definition that opposed independent publishing and transnationalization; but it is no longer a question of ownership, not even a question of the catalog, but rather of the construction of ties, affects, and complicities. And if it is about building communities, the work will never be perfect, and there will never be too many hands to do the work.

---

[33] Carolina Muzi "La cara y el cuerpo del libro: el trabajo de lxs diseñadorxs en la edición independiente" in Badenes and Stedile, *Estado de feria permanente*, 193-206.

[34] From 1976 to 1983 Argentina was ruled by a brutal military junta that killed or disappeared between 10,000 and upwards of 30,000 individuals, ostensibly to combat left-wing guerrilla movements but in practice targeting labor leaders, human rights activists, student organizers, and all others they could identify as left of the political center, as well as instituting wide-reaching censorship of news and culture and restricting civil and political rights. The dictatorship has continued to cast a shadow over Argentine democracy in the 40+ years since its end.

Bibliography

Astutti, Adriana and Sandra Contreras. "Editoriales independientes, pequeñas... micropolíticas culturales en la literatura argentina actual." *Revista Iberoamericana* 67, no. 197 (2001): 767-780.

Badenes, Daniel. "Comunicación e identidad en fábricas recuperadas-autogestionadas." Bachelor's thesis, Universidad Nacional de La Plata, 2005.

Badenes, Daniel. "Las revistas culturales como sector y como movimiento." In *Editar sin patrón. La experiencia política-profesional de las revistas culturales independientes*, edited by Daniel Badenes. La Plata: Club Hem, 2017.

Botto, Malena. "La concentración y la polarización de la industria editorial." In *Editores y políticas editoriales en Argentina, 1880-2000*, edited by J.L. de Diego. Buenos Aires: Fondo de Cultura Económica, 2006.

Botto, Malena. "Esos raros proyectos nuevos. Reflexiones para la conceptualización de las nuevas prácticas editoriales." Paper presented at the VIII Congreso Internacional de Teoría y Crítica Literaria Orbis Tertius, 2012.

Budassi, Sonia. "Los nuevos desafíos de la resistencia editorial." *Perfil*, August 10, 2008.

Colleu, Gilles. *La edición independiente como herramienta protagónica de la bibliodiversidad*. Buenos Aires: La marca editora, 2008.

De Diego, José Luis. "Concentración económica, nuevos editores, nuevos agentes." Paper presented in the Primer Coloquio Argentino del Libro y la Edición, La Plata, Argentina, 2012.

De Souza Muniz Júnior, José. "Itinerarios de una identidad voluble: el debate sobre la edición 'independiente' en Francia y Brasil." *Orbis Tertius* 20, no. 21 (2015): 145-158. https://www.orbistertius.unlp.edu.ar/article/view/OTv20n21a14.

García Espinosa, Julio. *Cine, comunicación y cambio social*. Lima: Editorial Causa Chun, 1989.

Gazzeram Carlos. *Editar—un oficio: Atajos/Rodeos/Modelos*. Villa María: EDUVIM, 2016.

Harari, Pablo. "La edición independiente en América Latina: un factor cultural en peligro." Paper presented in the Actas del 1er Encuentro de Editores Independientes de América Latina, 2000.

Hawthorne, Susan. *Bibliodiversidad: Un manifestó para la edición independiente*. Buenos Aires: La marca editora, 2018.

López Winne, Hernán and Víctor Malumián. *Independientes, ¿de qué?. Hablan los editores de América Latina*. Mexico City: Fondo de Cultura Económica, 2016.

Moscardi, Matías. *La máquina de hacer libritos. Poesía argentina y editoriales independientes en la década de los noventa*. Mar del Plata: Puente Aéreo, 2016.

Noël, Sophie. *La edición independiente crítica*. Villa María: EDUVIM, 2018.

Saferstein, Ezequiel. "La Feria del Libro Independiente y Autónoma (FLIA) en Buenos Aires. Tres ejes para su abordaje." *Argumentos. Revista de crítica social* 14 (2012). http://revistasiigg.sociales.uba.ar/index.php/argumentos/article/view/231.

Schierloh, Eric. "Sobre la independencia editorial (con coordenadas para evaluarla)." *Mimesis*, June 19, 2019, https://edicionesmimesis.cl/index.php/2019/06/29/sobre-la-independencia-editorial-con-coordenadas-para-evaluarla-por-eric-schierloh.

Schiffrin, André. *La edición sin editores*. Barcelona: Destino, 2000.

Seccia, Oriana. "Producciones artísticas independientes juveniles. Un pequeño tour problemático." *Solidaridad Global. Revista de la Universidad Nacional Villa María* 21 (2012): 81-86.

Stedile Luna, Verónica. "Formas de la crítica para nombrar una época." In *Editar sin patrón. La experiencia política-profesional de las revistas culturales independientes*, edited by Daniel Badenes. La Plata: Club Hem, 2017.

Szpilbarg, Daniela. "Escrituras permeables: la autogestión editorial en la literatura. El caso de Gordo de Sagrado Sebakis y En construcción de Pablo Strucchi." *Cuadernos LIRICO* 13 (2015). http://journals.openedition.org/lirico/2098.

Szpilbarg, Daniela and Ezequiel Saferstein. "El espacio editorial independiente: heterogeneidad, posicionamientos y debates. Hacia una tipología de las editoriales en el período 1998-2010." Paper presented at the Primer Coloquio Argentino de Estudios sobre el Libro y la Edición, 2012.

Tessio Conca, Eliana Silvia. "La edición independiente de libros. Estrategias comerciales de pequeñas editoriales en Paraná (Entre Rios) y los incentivos estatales para el sector en el período 2007-2013." Master's thesis, Universidad Nacional de Quilmes, 2017.

Vanoli, Hernán. "Pequeñas editoriales y transformaciones en la cultura literaria Argentina." *Revista Apuntes de Investigación del CECYP* 15 (2009): 161-185.

Vanoli, Hernán. "Sobre editoriales literarias y la reconfiguración de una cultura." *Nueva Sociedad* 230 (2010).

Vanoli, Hernán. *El amor por la literatura en tiempos de algoritmos. 11 hipótesis para discutir con editores, lectores, gestores y demás militantes*. Buenos Aires: Siglo XXI, 2019.

Vanoli, Hernán, and Ezequiel Saferstein. "Cultura literaria e industria editorial. Desencuentros, convergencias y preguntas alrededor de la escena de las pequeñas editoriales." In *Creatividad, economía y cultura en la ciudad de Buenos Aires, 2001-2010*, edited by Lucas Rubinich and Paula Miguel. Buenos Aires: Aurelia Rivera, 2011.

Winik, Marilina. "Experimento FLIA." Paper presented at the Jornadas Producción cultural, nuevos saberes e imaginarios en la sociedad argentina contemporánea a la luz de la globalización, Buenos Aires, Instituto de Investigaciones Gino Germani, 2010.

Zaid, Gabriel. *Los demasiados libros*. Barcelona: Anagrama, 2001.

Collaborative Distribution
Contingent Alliances and Consolidated Projects

Gustavo Velázquez

Translated by Jack Rockwell

> This chapter was originally published as chapter 17 in Daniel Badenes and Verónica Stedile Luna, eds. *Estado de feria permanente: La experiencia de las editoriales independientes argentinas, 2001-2020* (La Plata: Club Hem Editores, 2020), a collection of studies of independent publishing in Argentina produced by the "La edición en la era de redes" (Publishing in the Era of Networks) project at the Universidad Nacional de Quilmes in La Plata, Argentina. While focused specifically on Argentina, Velázquez's findings provide a rich, nuanced description, based on first-hand accounts, of the work independent publishers undertake to produce and distribute their publications, often at the edges of mainstream publishing markets. Editorial notes have been added for references to Argentine politics and history. The editors thank Badenes, Stedile, and the publishers at Club Hem for allowing us to publish this work in translation.

Collaboration appears as a common phenomenon in the contemporary publishing sector. Publishers come together to share information, to advise on emerging projects, to participate in book fairs under shared stands—or even to create their own book fairs. One of the shared problems that publishers have had to attend to is the question of distribution and sales.

Distribution is a structural problem[1] that has a considerable impact on small publishers, who must make efforts to acquire visibility and make themselves known in an environment made adverse by consolidation in the sector. It is a central task: each imprint's possibilities of sustenance, growth, and professionalization ultimately depend on it. This chapter will demonstrate some of the collaborative experiences of independent publishers that arise from facing up to problems of distribution and participation in fairs. It investigates the reasons that have motivated the formation of some distributors, such as Asunto Impreso, Como Cuatro, and Carbono; and the editorial collectives La Coop and Malisia. We also look at more unusual agreements, oriented towards participation in book fairs, following the experiences of Todo Libro es Político and Frente Mar. The unifying thread in all these cases is the conjunction of the efforts and perspectives on editorial activity that enrich its independent and self-managing sector.

On the road to self-distribution

Distribution is a fundamental stage in the value chain of the book industry. This work permits the circulation and presence of the texts at commercial points, in a way that influences possible sales.

In general terms, the principal activities entailed by distribution are *logistics* (storage, pickup, packaging, returns, billing and receipts) and *commercialization*, which includes marketing, promotion and pre- and post-sale services (Gil and Gómez, 2017).

Forms of distribution can be characterized, in broad strokes, as third-party distribution and self-distribution. Third-party distribution consists of working with a distribution services business. This means putting the books in the hands of a commercial firm that takes control of logistics, preparation and control of sales, and other such things. The function of this intermediary is to sell, move and place books within commercial channels. In exchange, the distributing firm receives a percentage of the sales of each product.

Self-distribution, as the name indicates, consists of performing these activities on one's own account. In such cases, these tasks and logistics

---

1   Note that distribution is a topic that has not been treated exhaustively in the fields of book studies and the study of publishing. The information presented here is a reconstruction of a series of interviews with independent publishers performed in 2016, 2017, and 2018.

are absorbed by the publisher itself. This is an extensive practice within independent publishers.[2] But the execution of distribution is not necessarily "individual": small and medium-sized undertakings have found a way to mitigate the structural difficulties of commercial circulation by means of alliances.

Asunto Impreso can be considered an antecedent to independent distributors. It emerged in 1995, created by Guido Indij:

> Asunto Impreso was born as the distribution business of a single imprint, La marca editora. Later it took on the distribution of other national and foreign imprints, as well as individual authors, and continued adding more catalogs. It was born as a means of independently negotiating commercial matters with bookstores. (Guido Indij, editor of La marca editora, 2018)

Currently, Asunto Impreso handles the distribution of La marca, Interzona, Factotum and Asunto Impreso Ediciones.[3] If this is not quite an experience of cooperation between publishers as such, this distributor is oriented towards the independent publishing sector, aiming to dedicate itself exclusively to these kinds of catalogs.

> We are not accepting more imprints, and we are not interested in growing at their expense. There are many distributors that take on more and more imprints in order to grow, but that doesn't mean that this growth is organic and that all of these imprints grow with the distributor. It sometimes happens that the imprints sell less while the distributor keeps growing. This is not what interests us. (Guido Indij, editor of La marca editora, 2018)

As Guido Ondij suggests, third-party distribution services often don't meet the needs of independent publishers. They accumulate many clients and, in practice, end up privileging the products of larger publishing houses. The reasoning is obvious: books that circulate quickly mean more profits for the bookstore and the distributor. Small publishers, on the other hand, don't generate bestsellers with sales

---

2   In the following chapter [number 18 in the volume *Estado de feria permanente*], Néstor González discusses the experiences of Las cuarenta with regards to this topic in greater detail.

3   A separate business than the distributor, in addition to the bookstore: Asunto Impreso Librería de la Imagen.

greater than 30,000 copies in a relatively short period of time: their titles require more time to position themselves in the market.

On the other hand, the context of consolidation influences the unequal conditions of distribution. This is because large businesses have a greater capacity to negotiate with commercial intermediaries, to generate discounts and acquire better displays in bookstores. This creates obstacles for projects of smaller economic scale that can't compete with the levels of profitability that the "majors" make available for distributors.

In independent experiences, activities oriented towards distribution have other ends. The objective is rather the positioning and commercial yield of the project itself; the distribution is basically an instrument in the service of the growth of the publishing house.

To this end, Coma Cuatro, the distributor of Caja Negra and Cactus, was formed around 2012. They also distribute materials by Cuenco de Plata to certain bookstores and geographic sectors. The initiative began with the participation of four publishing houses who had previous experience in self-distribution. After various internal changes, today the distributor is centered around the mentioned imprints:

> Sort of following from this experience of common spaces of dialogue which were set up around the Feria (La Feria Internacional del Libro de Buenos Aires), the possibility arose of working together on this problem that, generally speaking, all independent publishers have, whether small- or medium-sized, which is that of distribution. That's how the possibility came up, and little by little each of us started leaving behind the distribution systems we had at the time. We were beginning to imagine this thing and give it form. (Ezequiel Fanego, editor at Caja Negra, 2018)

This sharing of common activities came about as a result of meetings between editors. In this sense, book fairs are an important environment. As we'll see momentarily, the first experiences of collective management are expressed here, following from the communal purchase of stands by several imprints.

Coma Cuatro proposes a different model of a distribution services business. Ezequiel Fanego remarks that:

> By not considering distribution as a business in itself, it becomes a distribution that is conceived of in service of the needs of publishing houses. This brings us advantages with both costs and the

performance of each of the brands at bookstores. (Ezequiel Fango, editor at Caja Negra, 2018)

The scope of the distribution is at the service of the publishers, a situation that changes the logic of their commercial circulation. This takes the form of a series of administrative decisions and financial operations that contribute to the commercial performance of the distributed. So, for example, the distributor can reduce its costs to favor the distributed:

> Unlike when you work with other distributors, the percentage that the distribution takes isn't a fixed percentage for us. You work with a distributor and they charge you a fixed percentage, and this percentage contains their profits, which is variable, and variability, among other things, has to do with costs. The distributor sometimes manages to lower its costs and earn greater profits. This isn't always a function of selling more books, but is rather often related to other decisions that they have to take, such as warehousing, transportation, et cetera. In our case, the question of the percentage is different. What the publishers of our distribution company are charged per month is a variable cost with respect to the net cost. That is to say, there is no margin of financial gain for the distributor. If, for some reason, the distribution costs should be lower one month, the publishers would pay less and earn a higher percentage per sold book. (Ezequiel Fanego, editor at Caja Negra, 2018)

In this case, the profit margin of the distributor is minimal. Collective benefit drives the design. Distribution is no longer conceived as its own business, rather being thought of as an activity where yields are made collective.

Coma Cuatro distributes throughout the country [Argentina] to around 200 bookstores. Another advantage of forming an organization of this type has to do with greater attention paid to publishers' growth. This is achieved by careful work with their materials in commercial channels, that is only possible by means of diligence that the editors themselves can provide, as they know their own materials best and know which potential audiences to direct them towards. This is an added value that is registered at the moment of interaction with booksellers, whose relation becomes more direct and disintermediated.

La Coop is an association of independent publishers. It's composed of the following imprints: Alto Pogo, Años Luz, Audisea, Azul, Conejos,

China, Espacio Hudson, Mágicas Naranjas, Paisanita, ¿Qué diría Víctor Hugo?, Santos Locos, Clubcinco, Evaristo Editorial, and Clase Turista. The greatest work that La Coop does has to do with distribution. Even though La Coop recently extended its reach to include some publishers that are not members of the group, its distribution is especially oriented to its members' work.

> In reality, La Coop is, before being a distributor, a group of publishers, publishers who have come together to see how we might approach a process of collective work. Two key points that interested us were distribution and participation in book fairs. Alone, an imprint could work with some bookstores, could cover the costs of travel to some book fairs, but you couldn't cover the great range of fairs and the many bookstores that there are in Buenos Aires. So we began to wonder if we might not form our own distribution for these imprints, with the idea of creating a distributor that could then offer services to other publishers. This is what we're working on today. La Coop has been working for three years, and we've been oiling the gears of distribution work, as it has not been a short process, nor has it been easy. (Marcos Almada, editor at Alto Pogo, 2018)

The association allows them to take on sales spaces that one imprint by itself could not, in both national and foreign territories. Dialogue with booksellers is more efficient and strategic, with a view to better dissemination of each catalog.

Work is always in service of the collective good, for which reason the growth of the members is proportional to that of La Coop, which also has its own bookstore and organizes various cultural activities such as presentations, talks, and workshops. "What self-distribution gives us," affirms Marcos Almada, "is greater freedom when it's time to make decisions about where to send our books" (interview, 2018). This liberty alludes to the possibility of choosing which bookstores to work with, or even which publishers to work with. This translates to more efficient management of shipping and returns. Foregoing a contract with a distributor permits one to have control over commercial circulation. What's more, the cost usually destined to pay for distribution as a service can be applied to discounts and promotions in bookstores.

Similar to this experience is Malisia, a collective of La Plata-based publishers formed in 2013. The component publishers are EME, Club Hem, Malisia Editorial, and Pixel. The unified work of these actors has formed a circuit of production and dissemination of relevant books in the territory. About its beginnings, Agustín Arzac, an editor at EME, comments:

> We came from the experience of a magazine called Estructura Mental de las Estrellas, and from actively participating in FLIA de La Plata, which at this time was a very important meeting for independent publishers. In 2009 we began the magazine, and in 2012, three years later, we met the guys from Pixel and Club Hem, who were about to put out their first book. That's when we thought it was important to come together, as there were not many of us publishers from La Plata, and we were participating in street fairs and cultural activities and presentations, beginning to augment the work of each of our own imprints under a group which was collective, collaborative, and self-managed. That's how Malisia was born, with the intention of finding our own space in which we could work to sell our materials through a bookstore and also to start to distribute our materials, working together. (Agustín Arzac, editor at EME, 2018)

From that point on, they pooled the contacts that each of them had and began integrated distribution. In this way, they could arrive at all of their points of sale with more agility, keeping in mind that the distribution practiced by Malisia is especially focused on bookstores and other spaces in La Plata and Greater La Plata. For the rest of the country, the collective outsources the work to a third-party distributor, Waldhuter.

This condition serves as an example for thinking of a third possible model of distribution in which one combines one's own work with that of a third party. This mixed-character model is practiced by some independent publishers who self-distribute to some geographical zones or bookstores (by consignment or direct sale), and for others, contract with distribution services. The decision in these cases is a tactical one: on the one hand, this permits publishers to sustain a more personalized relationship with certain sales channels at the same time as the distributor facilitates expansion into other national or international territories; and on the other, it assures that one doesn't leave all of their materials in the hands of a distributor, and so avoids the problem of not knowing where one's own books are, and the consequent loss of copies.

Actions like these mitigate the risks inherent in extending a book's reach as widely as possible. Agustín Arzac considers that

> The greatest difficulties of distribution have to do with logistical costs. To send a package of books today to an interior province, such as Mendoza, for example, costs about $400, $500 [Argentine pesos], more or less. This makes distribution unsustainable, to an extent, as the books are sent on consignment, so perhaps we don't immediately receive the payback for the money spent on this package. In fact, it's a gamble to send out books like this. (Agustín Arzac, editor at EME, 2018)

As is known, the length of book supply chains makes economic returns on books take months to arrive. To take away the mediation of a distributor is to shorten these chains. Connections between publishers become an alternative to multiply the impact of each undertaking:

> Generating alliances with other publishers is at the heart of Malisia. That's how we came about, with the understanding that what we could each do separately would be irrelevant, almost invisible. And if we succeeded in generating a union between various publishers, at least in La Plata, we could have an impact. And I think that we achieved it, I think that now in the city there is a clear reference to what independent publishers are. And, within these independent publishers, there is an important group which is publishing and producing all the time, which is Malisia. (Agustín Arzac, editor of EME, 2018)

In addition to distribution, the collective does various things, including the management of El Espacio, a place where the Malisia bookstore is located and where other various cultural activities take place; and the organization of EDITA, the most important book fair featuring independent publishers in La Plata. Even though Malisia isn't incorporated as a cooperative, obtaining this legal status is an aspiration of the group.

The value of information

As we've said, the distributor is a mediator that receives copies of books and takes charge of their maintenance and storage; they prepare orders, handle packaging, boxing, transportation, verification of the accounts of booksellers and invoicing. They also manage books that are returned from points of sale (Colleu, 2008). For these reasons, they transmit information between the bookstore and the publishing house, with respect to the state of sales, as well as holding corresponding documents such as invoices, bills, and proofs-of-delivery. Here lies the reason why some independent presses have abandoned third-party distribution. Concretely, it was what motivated the creation of the distributor Carbono by Ediciones Godot and El Gourmet Musical. This firm also distributes Sigilo, but this publishing house is not a business that participates in the distributor's management decisions.

Carbono is the most recently started distributor discussed here: it began to function in 2017 and since it has been incorporated as a S.R.L. (Sociedad de Responsabilidad Limitada [similar to a U.S. Limited Liability Company]) since February 2018.

> I don't think anyone starts a publishing house wanting to get into distribution. Distribution is like a necessary evil. It's something that must be done, but it's not exciting to pack boxes, you do it because you have no choice. It's not exciting to count inventory, you do it because you have no choice. What it is, however, at least for us, is a one-way trip. Once you start to have all of this information, when you have direct contact with booksellers, when you can arrive at more places and when you know well what's happening with your books, you never want to go back, that would be crazy. It's lots of work, lots of labor, it wears you down, but it's good. (Víctor Malumián, editor of Ediciones Godot, 2018)

The information that Malumián is referring to, and that distributors often retain, allows one to know what bookstores their books are in, how many copies are in stock, and in which bookstores one title performs better than another. To have control over this information makes for a more efficient management of distribution that can result in, for example, taking books out of one bookstore where they're not selling well, and attending with more detail to commercial points where your catalog has higher turnover, and avoid loss of stock.

When a restocking order doesn't arrive on time, sales are lost. In the third-party model, the bookstore's losses pass first to the distributor and then to the editor. Along this trajectory months can go by before copies arrive at bookstores, and sales fall. With one's own distribution, on the other hand, these actions can occur more immediately so that the cycle of demand that a given title traverses isn't lost.

On the other hand, distribution is a demanding task. The work that this activity requires forces editors to divide themselves between the roles of editing, administration and finances. In this sense, when the structure grows it becomes crucial to take on personnel. Of the cases mentioned here, Asunto Impreso, Coma Cuatro and Carbono have employees dedicated exclusively to distribution. Nonetheless, it is the editors who coordinate and make administrative decisions.

In other cases, it is the editors themselves who take on the work of distribution. This leads to the accumulation of activities that have more to do with the commercial aspects of books than the intellectual work more properly of an editor. Self-distribution, in these cases, supposes a quantity of time dedicated to circulation "con mochila"—with a bag on the shoulder. For it is not a logistics that requires fleets or massive infrastructure, but one accomplished on foot, on buses, subways, personal cars, et cetera. This mode of distribution, by going to bookstores with restocking orders of two or three copies, is part of the self-managing activity that demands intensive dedication by editors.

Participation in Book Fairs

Participation in book fairs is another face of commercial distribution. They are a very important channel in which independent publishers have also applied collective strategies to make their presence felt. Just as distributors have been constituted, there are substantial possibilities for collaborative experiences. To this respect, it's common that editors form groups to share stands at fairs. Todo Libro es Político is just this: an alliance that was born to facilitate participation in the Feria Internacional del Libro de Buenos Aires.

> Those of us who more or less put this together are Matías Reck of Milena Cacerola; Marilina Winik of Hekht; Andrés Barconi and Javier Benderski of Tinta Limón; and myself of La Cebra. We went to the fair called Encuentro Federal de la Palabra which happened at Tecnópolis, I think in 2015. We were at this fair where there was nobody, very few people. We found it really difficult to sell our books. This was in March. At the end, it occurred to me that we needed a stand at the Feria del Libro, and we only had about ten days to put it together. So we called the foundation and looked at the stands that were available. There was a 4x4 stand and we bought it. And it went really well, we sold more than 1,000 books. So it began. (Cristóbal Thayer, editor at La Cebra, 2018)

Since then, Todo Libro es Político's space has seen sustained growth that can be expressed by the number of its participants. The stand is divided between the eight members of the collective and each space, in turn, can be fragmented to accommodate more publishers. This makes it such that within the environment of Todo Libro es Político it is possible to find the material of nearly 20 different imprints: publishers that, were they alone, would not be able to participate in events like the FIL Buenos Aires. As Cristóbal Thayer explains, the objective is to create a space *that functions like a fair within the fair*:

> The high costs of the stands make it difficult for imprints to participate individually. This condition gives rise to diverse ways of trying to get around it. What I noticed is that there was a great imbalance, in the sense that the stand was expensive. You had to pay for the lot, build it, pay wages, pay for a whole bunch of things. And when it was time to split up the costs, everyone paid the same. Those of us who sold less, and we really sold very little, ended up financing those who sold more. So we came up with a model that was exactly the opposite. The idea is that we prorate all of the costs of the stand according to sales. So if you sell 30, you pay 30. It's a model that can only succeed. What happens is that each book that is sold, is sold with the same discount. When you do your final accounts, of a book of yours that sold 10 copies and a book of mine that sold 50, each book has the same discount. This is to make sure that no one is going to burn books at the fair.
>
> Every year, everyone leaves very happy. It was a success in the sense that of the 100% of the cover price of a book, the cost was no more than 60%. So if you did this, all was good, but if not you're burning part of the book. And if you break even, you're burning the whole book. You went to the fair, you did everything, you worked really hard and you have 100, 200, 300 books less. That there is a loss. At Todo Libro es Político this doesn't happen. Tinta Limón sold many books this year, 25% of the stand, and Cebra sold 5% of the stand, and each of these books has the same dignity, in a way. There are no first- and second-place books. (Cristóbal Thayer, editor at La Cebra, 2018)

Agreements between publishers also allow discounts, promotions and other commercial, artistic and political activities to be put into practice. One that's well-recognized is the initiative promoted by Todo Libro es Político for 2-for-1 book sales during the Feria de Buenos Aires in 2017. Under the slogan "2x1 para los libros, perpetua para los genocidas" [2x1 for books, life term for genocide], the promotion was launched in repudiation of the ruling of the Argentine Supreme Court of Justice that ordered that the 2x1 law be applied to those convicted of crimes against humanity. Other stands such as La Coop, Sólidos Platónicos, and La Sensación, and the imprint Mardulce, also joined in this promotion.

That communion between editors is a constant in the world of book-fairs is clearly evidenced by the example of Todo Libro es Político. They seek to make benefits mutual in these environments that can only be tackled by collective means. If they didn't, certain editors would be kept out of these commercial circuits by the impossibility of covering costs.

Outside of Buenos Aires, we can find the experience of collectives of independent publishers in the example of Córdoba's Frente Mar. This collective was composed of Llanto de Mudo, Editorial Nudista, Los Ríos Editorial, Pan Comido, La Sofía Cartonera, Ediciones de la Terraza, Dínamo Poético, Ediciones Documenta Escénicas, Letra Nómada, and Borde Perdido Editora. Tamara Pachado, editor at Los Ríos Editorial, affirms:

> We editors know each other, we cross paths. We see the material that each of us has, the catalog, what their circuit of bookstores is, which are not all the same. We always have the same difficulties trying to grow our distribution, the commercial circuit. So we started to have some meetings, coming from some discussions that we had with the city regarding our participation in book fairs. This put us more in contact with one another, and we found a certain affinity in this group, which is the publishers that finally formed Frente Mar. We are more or less homogenous with regards to the level of production and our intentions to work collectively. So we began to meet often over several months, until the idea for Frente Mar finally emerged. (Tamara Pachado, editor of Los Ríos Editorial, 2018)

So Frente Mar was born to strengthen the commercialization of independent imprints of Córdoba. Participation in book fairs requires the same logistics as working with bookstores: packing boxes, moving them, traveling.

> Frente Mar has as its principal objective to work together to grow the circuit of distribution of all of the editors that form it. But this was no more than an additional workload, even greater than what we already had as editors. Unless someone could take charge of the traveling. So we put together something like a mini-warehouse, a mini-consignment that moved all around and if someone, outside of those three people who were in charge of doing it, had an invitation or a chance to participate somewhere else, they did it and the books were moved. This was the initial project. It lasted for two years, and it went really well. (Tamara Pachado, editor of Los Ríos Editorial, 2018)

Logistics is a matter that's alleviated when its burden is shared by many. The division of tasks is a positive factor at the time of moving boxes, or even attending the stand. This last task, for example, means the investment of many hours. Some hire a fair worker, but in the majority of cases it is the editors themselves who take turns covering the space, and so no one has to take away too much time from their usual work.

Frente Mar was discontinued in 2016. The burden of its activities became such that it was not possible to sustain the association. Even though the collective no longer exists, it contributed to the recognition of independent publishers in Córdoba, the links between the editors remain and, on occasion, their reunions have had a special political impact.[4]

All of the publishers mentioned in this chapter participate in book fairs with shared stands. Cost often determines the possibility of participating in book fairs, national as well as international. Working together, it's possible to bring these costs down, in case the numbers don't add up for the editors.

The environment of book fairs is a seedbed from which joint projects and ideas emerge. The meetings between editors give rise to collaborations which indicate the strengthening of the sector, more so than isolated projects. These kinds of networks nourish and give meaning to the editorial field.

Final reflections

The visibility of a book depends to a great extent on the capacity of commercial distribution, and this activity is found to be connected to the economic scale of the businesses. This puts the smallest at a disadvantage, who resort to alternative methods to supplant these shortcomings. To the extent that it interferes with the circulation of books, it affects the cultural sphere. Distribution defines which books arrive at readers and which do not, in a way that has inevitable repercussions on bibliographic diversity. This variable cannot be left un-analyzed, even if it implies detours through processes that, at first sight, appear

---

4   One fruit of these reunions has been the creation of the space Barón Biza. This stand is paid for by the city, and every year makes a selection of independent publishers to assure that they can participate in the Feria del Libro de Córdoba: "Barón Biza continues to be for us today a great space and a great achievement. It has been amply recognized by the community of Córdoba. It is the most valuable space in the Fair because it's the one that really has the support of the editors of Córdoba" (Tamara Pachado, editor of Los Ríos Editorial, 2018).

to be technical and logistical. The economic criteria of distribution can prevent certain books from reaching their potential readers.

The decision to take on distribution speaks to the grade of professionalization that independent editors have acquired of late. Self-distribution is presented as an alternative to shore up commercialization, which many small imprints opt for. The jump in terms of results can be significant; however, the line between thriving and surviving becomes thin in distribution. To put together a logistical structure is costly, and often means taking resources away from, or at least sharing them with, other activities.

This is where publisher's collectives have gained importance. Collective formations contribute to amplifying visibility, increasing sales, and solving certain difficult problems such as participation in book fairs or keeping accounts open with certain bookstores. At the same time, these experiences strengthen the ecosystem of communications around books.

Associations are born, disappear, and transform into other associations. Groups are formed, and some cooperatives appear, but spontaneous agreements prevail. It's more and more common that editors come together in meetings, between groups and within each organization. As if they were plenary sessions, common problems and collective solutions are discussed at these times. Among these actors, a generalized knowledge exists of the necessity to unite before imbalances generated by the market.

Bibliography

Colleu, Gilles. *La edición independiente como herramienta protagónica de la bibliodiversidad*. Buenos Aires: La marca editora, 2008.

Gil, Manuel and Martín Gómez. *Manual de edición: guía para estos tiempos revueltos*. Buenos Aires: La mara editora, 2017.

What is an Independent Publisher?

La Furia del Libro

Translated by Lisa Gardinier

> La Furia del Libro is a collective of Chilean independent publishers which also coordinates a book fair by the same name since 2009. La Furia del Libro (literally, the fury of the book) is a play on words with "feria del libro," or book fair, and was organized in response to independent publishers marginalized by the Cámara Chilena del Libro, the mainstream Chilean publishing organization, and the Santiago International Book Fair. As of 2023, La Furia organizes events in June and December, with over 260 publishers at the June 2023 event. As in most other Latin American book fairs, readers can purchase directly from publishers.
>
> The following essay was written by the leadership of La Furia del Libro and published in the opinion section of *El Mostrador*, a Chilean online news site, on 4 December 2013, shortly before their then-annual book fair.

An independent publisher is an initiative of one or more people coming together to build a catalog that is, above all, a cultural contribution.

Although some of these initiatives include books written by the members of the editorial board, who in many cases are writers or content creators, an independent publisher is characterized by also including works by other authors outside of the publisher's editorial board. This differentiates it from a self-publishing press, in which the editor almost exclusively publishes books of their own authorship. In this sense, an independent publisher fulfills a social role by offering authors an opportunity to make their work known.

An independent publisher, in most cases, is funded by the contributions of the people who create it. Presses can receive support from non-profit institutions as long as those institutions are neither part of the independent publisher's structure nor require reimbursement of their investments. Just as the resources of an independent publisher come from its creators, an independent publisher maintains the autonomy of its catalog: it does not act on commercial or economic impulses, nor for the dissemination of creeds, religions, or spiritual leaders, but rather to the need to put into circulation genres, themes, styles, and formats that are not valued by other publishing projects for not being profitable. An independent publisher does not place financial results above cultural values, but it is not blind in this aspect either: these projects need resources to grow or continue, so revenue is not unwelcome.

From this point, we can deduce another trait of independent publishers: marketing expenses are very low or non-existent, replacing advertising expenses with active distribution and promotion work that is not reflected in the price of the books. The retail price of each title is an important issue for independent publishers, and that is why many of them are in favor of having a fixed cover price, which allows them to avoid mark-ups by distributors and retailers. During La Furia del Libro, many publishers are able to lower their prices and thus achieve higher levels of dissemination to readers.

Finally, an independent publisher takes care of local needs. They prioritize in their catalogs the expression of their home country: poetry, narrative, essay, chronicle, testimony, and all the genres that make up the memory of a country. This does not mean that an independent publisher avoids publishing foreign authors, but quite the opposite: it aims to increase the circulation of books in its production territory, and thus enrich the bibliodiversity of national literary resources.

Otras Formas
Case Studies

Queering Digital Publishing
Publishing Practices by Puntos Suspensivos

gaita nihil

Translated by Allison Stickley

My name is gaita nihil. I am a trans man, and I am the director of puntos suspensivos ediciones. We are an independent publisher located in Buenos Aires that publishes individuals from the LGTB+ community, specifically trans, *travesti*,[1] and non-binary people in the Spanish language. We focus on poetry but we also publish narratives and essays, with the intention of generating networks of employment (illustrators, editors, booksellers, other publishers, etc.) and cooperation among people in our community.

I would like to take this opportunity to talk about the democratization of culture and digital books. Specifically, the PDF, despite often not being considered valid as a digital book, is a format which allows for the democratization of culture. We can think of culture as a wide social attitude, a combination of customs and traditions within a geo-political environment that allows for the interpretation and reproduction of the world. We know some marginalized communities are found—we find ourselves—in a private and difficult position to access some features of culture. The difficulties can come from simply being

---

1 Translator's note: the term travesti refers to effeminate men and men who dress in women's clothing. The term, traditionally used as a pejorative, has recently been going through a process of reclaiming among the travesti community.

minorities or can cut across class. When considering minorities or sectors of society which are not valued, I think, for example, about people of sexual or gender dissidence, like trans*, *travestis*, non-binary folks. I also think about communities of senior citizens and about people with disabilities.

During the months of the pandemic and obligatory preventative social isolation, it was very important to note how digital publications in Argentina, and the PDF in particular, took on great prominence in distributing the culture we have access to.

As an example, I want to talk to you about Rosa Rodríguez Cantero's book. She is a 75-year-old author that publishes with us, and our publication is the digital version of "Lo senil no quita lo caliente" (Senility Doesn't Stop Horniness), a book of poetry about sex and love in old age, which also adds a sexually diverse point of view.

It was very important for us to lay out a digital book in PDF format because it was a form which readers from other provinces can access. Rosa is a poet and is invited to many provinces because she takes a humorous approach to senior citizens' sexuality. This is why it seems important to us that the books can reach readers who aren't from Buenos Aires. The importance of the PDF or the advantage I find in the PDF, is that it is a very light-weight book in which colors can be taken advantage of, compared to the EPUB, in which the background is changed according to the application or device being used. In this way we can creatively exploit colors and other resources, which we will see later.

In this format we replace the information present in the physical book, including the cover. We can also see our particular political stance, which is that the book is interactive and that we allow reproduction of the book, meaning we believe a person who pays for the book should have it and be able to present it like any other physical printed book. This is the difference when using other platforms like Bajalibros,[2] in which you have to have a username and password to access the book.

In this sense, once payment is received, we send the book by mail via our virtual sales platform. This supports the democratization of culture, particularly right now.

---

2   www.bajalibros.com

For us, it seems relevant to be able to reach as many people as possible and is fairly accessible in physical format, even in the case that people don't pay for the book. Considering that it is a community of trans* or retired people who generally find it difficult to buy a book, we wanted to create a product in this particular format for which only having a cell phone would be sufficient. We can take advantage of this by including some photographs or some extra material from talks the author was invited to.

In the end, we usually put current information regarding the moment in which the book was produced in the colophons, which is a guideline we usually put together with the authors.

We believe that collectivizing art, collectivizing culture and politics, is how we can construct a more interesting, richer and stronger way of publishing, and not just thinking about publishing books as a business in which it is what we more or less want to make as cultural producers, but also to be able to establish a network of policies and of sentiments which are in agreement with what we are distributing. I think this is one of the biggest tasks that has been given to independent publishers in recent years, which puntos suspensivos ediciones is a product of, from where it originated, and it is very interesting to know that we still have tools that allow communal and collective reproduction of our culture.

gaita nihil

- www.puntossuspensivosediciones.com.ar
- IG   https://www.instagram.com/puntossuspensivosediciones/
- FB   www.facebook.com/puntossuspensivosediciones
- YT   https://www.youtube.com/channel/UC1n6PG1pO8BfVES9hq0UcJw

Breaking Through the Heteropatriarchal Barriers
Rebel Publishing Paths

Rosa Serna

Translated by Allison Stickley

I have been working in the self-managed publishing world for about seven years. It is not THE publishing world with capital letters but a small world, that space where we start without knowing exactly what we are doing. Rehearsing. I like this idea, to think of the attempts as rehearsal, to build spaces that make sense to us. There is nothing finished, answers given, only rehearsals where we learn, cry, enjoy, grow, and in the best of cases, build small slits from which to look and position ourselves differently.

For me, editing is a process of doing, of creating, of questioning. Put stories into circulation, to open what is closed, to maintain the cracks. The systems of oppression are continually closing worlds, possibilities, discourses, escapes, closing any possibility of a destabilizing dialogue. Any gesture that tries to break the false secrecy that seeks to maintain itself at all costs is suspect. I would like to contribute to publishing a widening, a closure of what is closed, to stop maintaining the borders that separate us and make it impossible for us to listen, look, feel, think from other more terrifying coordinates for power.

I want to continue working from books, promoting encounters. I think it is the way I have found to open and spit on the walls that are imposed on us, to lift the lacerating and daily passages of good manners and common sense that silence our looks, narratives, and ways of feeling the world. The everyday that lacerates because it cannot be named, that hurts in the deepest depths because the same wound has passed through the same place an infinity of times and there is no way to point it out, to name it, to push it away because good manners and common sense prevent it from happening, it does not exist. The heteropatriarchal world is completely closed to the experience that we as women and dissidents have of the world.

I want books, reflections, and publishers to question, open up, create other horizons, and the internal practices that accompany this crack to in turn lead to widening it beyond and beyond the books. I want to start with a journey, the journey that has led me to where I am now and that I feel is like an open field, like a space of the possible. Space that is made with various narratives, with multiple tasks, with collective reflections and with publishers in rebellion that break the cis-heteropatriarchal fence that only sows death. I want to point out these journeys that make me see the political in publishing and understand the feminist publication as a political practice of the possible.

In Abya Yala[1] there is a strong publishing movement linked to social movements. Some publishers perhaps naming themselves from the notion of independents,[2] others without being positioned under that name are more linked to autonomous movements and what they represent in terms of outlook and critical political positioning. Magalí Rabasa, in *The Book in Movement: Autonomous Politics and The Lettered City Underground* defines these types of publishers as those that face or seek to create alternatives to the hierarchical and colonial knowledge of the modern book in order to destabilize these forms of knowledge/power. In this sense, the edition is linked to the social movement and is part of it, a tool born with and acquired through meaning from this space. In the author's words:

> The organic book is not a modification of the modern book but rather a book that challenges (or has the potential to challenge) the very notion of Eurocentric modernity through its interaction with collectively imagined and executed anti-capitalist, anti-state, anti-authoritarian,

---

1   Editors' note: Abya Yala is an Indigenous name for the Americas.

2   In this text I do not enter the discussion about independent publishers but I distance myself from this definition given that I find that the only thing that demarcates them from belonging to the big conglomerates is that they do not look to challenge the system but rather find a niche within it.

anti-patriarchal, and anti-colonial practices. I want to insist on the potential because what is at stake is, of course, not a completely or purely transformed or transformative object, but one that represents an attempt to bring about a different kind of encounter, one that critically acknowledges the relational privileges that have historically been linked to the book-object. In this sense, the organic book is an autonomous object that emerges not from institutional dynamics and structures (nor from a single individual author) but from collective practices of experimentation and becoming.[3]

In this sense, the book and its practices not only recognize the colonial and modern traits from which they come and the trajectory as an indoctrination device, but also subvert it with practices and forms by transforming the object itself. It would be an object that is filled with sense and significance as a result of the practices that give it materiality and consistency. So here centrality would be found in doing and the ways of doing. As part of the ARRE network (Amorosa y Rebelde Red de Editoriales or loving and rebellious network of publishers) I see an affinity in this description with the work that not only we do, but also that various publishers have been doing throughout history. There has always been a leak in the closed systems of literate cities and colonial books. I think there is a long history of editions that subvert the capture machine that is the colonial book and put dissident imaginaries and ideas into circulation which break the flow of Euro-centered, capitalist, heteropatriarchal, and colonial knowledge. These forms of publishing have existed since the beginning, and it is about tracing the paths they have left in order to continue expanding and multiplying them. Here I do not intend to make a genealogy of underground books and the practices and relationships they have made possible, but to start from where I live and the rehearsals that we are still doing to position the edition from a destabilizing political task.

When I speak of autonomous or feminist-antiracist publishing, I think that I am placing myself in an unfinished discussion, where these terms have not been conclusively established, despite the fact there are several experiences of alternative publishers that could fit within these parameters. Therefore, I want to mainly start from the reflections and dialogues between the publishers that make up ARRE (Amorosa

---

3   Magalí Rabasa, *The Book in Movement: Autonomous Politics and the Lettered City Underground* (Pittsburgh: University of Pittsburgh Press, 2019), 14.

y Rebelde Red de Editoriales), which are: Ediciones la Social (Mexico City), Kalicabra (Mexico City), Fusilemos la Noche (Oaxaca), and La Reci (San Cristóbal de las Casas, Chiapas). We are mixed collectives whose themes and forms of publication are similar. Our texts and foundation are based in learning from feminism and dissidence, autonomous struggles, anti-capitalist movements, anti-racism, adherence to the sixth declaration of the Selva Lacandon and decolonial thought.

Our horizon is autonomy, and books and publishing are tools to build it collectively in everyday life. We understand our forms and editing choices from a feminist and decolonial perspective. We have not reflected on what feminist publication implies and means nor on naming ourselves as such, but we have asked ourselves about the feminist publishing task in mixed collectives. However, we have not reached conclusions or systematized our dialogues and reflections because we have not had enough time given the constant need to materially maintain projects, all stemming from self-management.

The reflections we have made as La Reci have led us to name ourselves as an autonomous publisher because we believe that we must put adjectives to our political objective: autonomous, anti-patriarchal, anti-racist. We know that all publishing is political which is why we have to work towards a clear horizon based on concrete practices which materialize those adjectives. The decisions of what to publish and how to do it—from where—are central. For us, it is essential to put practices at the center: what, how, and for whom we are publishing. We have to question our own organization of work, our own ways, because otherwise the reasoning is the same and we end up being a niche neoliberal publisher. Autonomy is necessarily built collectively for us. It is to take the world in our hands to transform it, to be able to decide on our actions at each step, to build horizons of social transformation that do not remain in the discourse, to walk in step with practice. We learn every day, we do workshops, we rotate responsibilities, and little by little we are building a place of autonomy that is never an end point but rather a horizon that moves us. We are on the way to something more collective: a "common" project that can be called Colectivo La Reci. To this end, we have also built close relationships with several "independent" publishers and bookstores in Mexico and other countries such as Spain, Argentina, Chile, Guatemala, and the United States. We have gone through multiple transitions: from not having a store and being just a publisher, to opening a store, being a workshop, being a publisher, having online sales, starting to transition into distribution. We started with a lot of turmoil. The experience has given us grounds to think about what we understand as autonomy, towards where we project the idea going beyond the publisher and transcending towards the collective construction of transformation.

As part of the history and network of ARRE, it is important to mention Pensaré Cartoneras, a collective of which I was also a part. A publishing house which has stopped its work but was fundamental in the process of La Reci. Pensaré is a cartonera publishing project where, in addition to editing, we held workshops, presentations, meetings, and fairs. We edited a text about this collective, Cartonear es camino: Memoria colectiva a 5 años de editorial colectivo y re-equilibrios anticoloniales (Collective Memory After 5 years of Collective Publishing and Anti-colonial Re-balancing) that was also published by the same publisher (2019). This project puts touch as an essential part of the practice of making books and listening as a necessary construction space to do collective work.

These small biographical notes are examples that lead me to think about publishing from a place in motion which they create in the collective and whose horizon is autonomy. Autonomy more as a practice than as a concept. Here again I return to the book by Magalí Rabasa where, based on the definition of autonomy of the collective situations, she says:

> ...a situated practice-concept that can only be understood in terms of *doing* (as in collective action), rather than as an idea or theory to be applied. This emphasis on *doing* underscores the contingent and processual nature of autonomy as a never-fulfilling political and social aspiration. In this sense it is more a "horizon of desire" (Gutiérrez Aguilar, 2008b), a becoming, and "an organization of hope" rather than a fixed state.[4]

An edition where doing and forms are central. Where there is an open process that is questioned, that seeks to inhabit differently and produce worlds with the book as a pretext but also as a tool. Not a space for the perpetuation of a knowledge that indoctrinates, but a possibility of thinking about knowledge in the plural, in collective doing, in the future of movements and life. A knowledge, as Adriana Guzmán would

---

4   Rabasa, 51; citing Raquel Gutiérrez Aguilar.

say, useful for the life and struggle of peoples. A book which seeks to share useful reflections for social transformation, and not only that, but also seeks, in the very process of materializing as a book, to generate and build relationships, connections, ways of doing that break the reproduction of a hierarchical, colonial, capitalist, and heteropatriarchal social order. Thus, the book space becomes one more trench to add to these social transformations which have been dreaming and walking from various fields.

Another form of alternative publishing that has had great repercussions in the alternative publishing world is the zine. Regarding the theoretical production on this movement linked to feminism and the role of women in publishing, it is essential to mention Gelen Jeleton, Andrea Galaxina or Andrea Díaz Cabezas, and Patricia Pietrafesa since they have all been involved with zine work and, in turn, they have written and theorized about it from their own practice.

Gelen Jeleton carried out the DIY archival work described in "Una archiva del DIY (Do It Yourself): Autoedición y autogestión en artivismo feminista; entre anarchivos sentimentales y cuir" (A DIY archive: Self-publishing and management in feminist artivism, between sentimental and queer anarchives, 2016).[5] In it she outlines the history of the zine through research into its background and meaning, as well as its roots in the punk movement. Jeleton focuses on the production of feminist zines and covers the history of the Riot Grrrl movement. The archive builds from a feminist-queer framework and documents different creators from whom Jeleton collected and includes the creation of new content in which she herself participates. In addition, her work continues with the ongoing expansion of the archive and its exhibition in spaces from fairs to museums. Jeleton's work is highly relevant due to its compilation methodology, the genealogy it builds, and the dissemination it mobilizes. Another important systematization work on zines is that of Andrea Galaxina who is part of the Bombas para Desayunar (Bombs for Breakfast) publishing house and has an essential publication on zine production made by women in the Kingdom of Spain: "I can say what I want, I can do what I want."[6] There she makes a

---

[5] Gelen Jeleton (María Ángeles Alcántara Sánchez), "Una archiva del DIY: Autoedición y autogestion en artivismo feminista; entre anarchivos sentimentales y cuir," *Panorama*, 2, 2016, 119-130. http://doi.org/10.30827/5053

[6] Andrea Galaxina, *Puedo decir lo que quiera! Puedo hacer lo que quiera! Una genealogía incompleta del fanzine hecho por chicas* (Madrid: Bombas para Desayunar, 2017).

brief tour of women in culture, feminism, and the influence of Riot Grrrl and Ladyfests in Spain. She, in turn, recounts the production and beginnings of Grrrl zines in Spain.

For her part, Patricia Pietrafesa is part of the zine publishing house Alcohol y Fotocopias (Alcohol and Photocopies) in Argentina and is one of the promoters of the punk book fair in Argentina. In addition, she is a zine maker, feminist, punk, and cumbia dancer. Pietrafesa compiled the history of the punk movement in Argentina in the book *Resistencia. Registro impreso de la cultura punk rock subtearránea, Buenos Aires 1984-2001* (*Resistance: Printed Record of Underground Punk Rock Culture, Buenos Aries 1984-2001*, 2013). An important part of her zine collection is present in the book. In her words:

> I wanted not only to compile the zines that I had made in all those years, but also to include some columns I wrote for *Rebelión Rock* and *Máximo Rock and Roll* to thus be able to give my vision of the scene I had lived. I am passionate about history, and I have a lot of archives, and I understood it was something I had to tell. I think it is a good contribution on my part and contribution, making the archive available to whoever wants to read it.[7]

Piertrafesa has also done other work of collecting zines, sharing her own archive to record and disseminate the history of zines in Argentina (she participates in the Archivo Culturas Subterráneas collective, a project to catalog alternative and peripheral cultural productions). In addition, the publishing house that she founded, Alcohol y Fotocopias, published the book *Homoxidal 500* (2016), a recuperation of dissident punk zines from Buenos Aires from 2001 to 2003.[8] She continues to do editorial work with zines and books as well as be part of the musical group Kumbia Queers.

It is worth noting, that at this intersection of punk, feminism, and zines, is the Riot Grrrl movement. What is interesting for me about this movement, is that publishing is thought of from feminism in a very concrete way, linking feminism, publishing, and counterculture; becoming, therefore, a reference to think about these intersections.

---

7   Interview with Sebastián Ramos in Patricia Pietrafesa, *Resistencia: Registro impreso de la cultura punk rock subterránea, Buenos Aires, 1984-2001* (Buenos Aires: Alcohol & Fotocopias, 2013).

8   Rafael Aladjem, ed., *Homoxidal 500: Fanzines, 2001-2003* (Buenos Aires: Alcohol & Fotocopias, 2016).

Furthermore, it goes beyond the act of making books and becomes a movement. Riot Grrrl emerged in the Global North from the women linked to the punk movement. One of the emblematic groups of this movement is Bikini Kill, with the figure of Kathleen Hanna leading. They sought to respond and confront the misogyny within the punk movement relating to heteropatriarchal norms, and build alternative spaces within the critical world of music. "Women to the front" was a cry that led to women occupying spaces in the concerts from which they were previously displaced. Punk is a protest movement, critical and disbelieving in the movement of progress and good manners that in those times sought to totalize spaces and consciences. Punk is built from the underground as a movement among dissatisfied youth who express their dissatisfaction with their clothing, codes, and music. But, as it is usual to find in other spaces, the criticism does not reach the heteropatriarchy that is also reproduced within these struggles and movements. Riot Grrrl says "Stop it!" to this.

A movement that explicitly relates punk to feminism and the publishing world is the philosophy of do it yourself or do it with others. It brings with it an aesthetic of access to the means of production and creative work where experience and self-knowledge are central elements that collapse the distinction between the personal and the political. It was an invitation for women to tell their stories, stories of sexual abuse and violence, from stereotypical to the most explicit physical violence. It was an exchange of words, feelings, a desire to share oneself with others and circulate stories that went through each one. The zines were mainly self-referential matters that invited love between women in the face of the rivalry proposed by the system. They put sexual abuse, compulsory and compulsive heterosexuality, and domestic abuse on the table and include the notion that the personal is political, which arises from a specific social and ideological context. It criticizes the social restrictions of the possible. In particular, it gives an account of the intimate as a premise to revisit the house, the family, the body, as vectors of power and places for the normalization of violence.

Confessional performance, especially in zines, becomes part of the intimate culture that gives weight to the personal revolution by exposing themselves as full of flaws and in process, puts those who are privileged up for examination. In this sense, there are two important criticisms that have been made of the movement. On the one hand, the criticism of its intimate side, which can be seen in parallel to the women's circles of the 70s—interesting and important spaces for raising awareness—seems to be exhausted in this space of intimacy without having built a wider socio-organizational response. The danger of this is staying trapped in the individual and not positioning oneself in a broader and more structural context and therefore failing to create more complex responses to a world which is sustained by multiple and intricate systems of oppression. On the other hand, despite the discussion of privilege and the awareness of racism, there continued to be a white bias within the movement. These are two important issues to consider when we revisit this movement, which did not last long but whose spirit rippled outward in a scenario that needed critical review of heteropatriarchy and misogyny in the countercultural movement. The exclusion of racialized women was a critical flaw, though they too are part of the story in breaking down heteropatriarchal barriers.

At this point it is important to consider geopolitics and its relationship with the territories where the production of books or zines is more profuse and the work they have done is more widespread. In this sense, the historically privileged spaces for the production of books in Spanish are Spain and Argentina. It is no coincidence that these are the places with a high number of jobs and alternative publishing processes, including self-management and feminist. I believe these resistances within the hegemonic spaces are important to mention, not to continue with a narrative that perpetuates these geographies as publishing meccas, but to contrast them and show what is being done from the "cultural cradles" in terms of opening cracks in the issue. On the other hand, the United States is an interesting case in terms of zines due to the number of subalternized groups that have used subalternity as a tool of resistance. This is the case of Riot Grrrl, but also many others. I put these geographies with their examples to generate a map, very preliminary of course, from the cracks that have left halos which continue to affect the narratives of alternative publishing and wanting, of course, to extend these genealogies from other references and territories. For now, I will mention just a couple more publishers found through my own personal journey as an editor, and admitting that I still have a lot to discover in different reference project geographies in this path of feminist publishing work and others.

Feminist publishers may have come into existence more explicitly in recent times. Of these I want to mention a project that has been and is fundamental for me and my understanding of publishing from feminism and anti-racism. This project is based in Chile and is a small publishing house called FEA (Feminismos, Estrías y Autogestión or feminisms, stretch marks, and self-management). It was created around the year 2015 by Gabriela Contreras. From that moment, the project has expanded to serve as a home for sexual dissident writers. Furthermore, in the words of Gabriela:

> we decided to work with authors from the African diaspora. Our interest is talking about a feminism that opposes racism, colonialism, and patriarchal concepts; we work on essays and poetry, and we want to open up new fields of research. We are interested in generating discussion around getting to know each other, knowing what our origins are and not ignoring who we are.[9]

This project works from self-management, radical tenderness, and rage. Texts with an anti-racist feminist perspective are distributed. In the words of those who are part of FEA, "we seek to raise a question, around the visible bodies of the feminist project. We want to be loud within the white, skinny, straight mandate. We are anti-racist and anti-colonial feminist writers" (from the FEA Facebook @FEAEDITORIAL). This is a publishing body that starts from the body, the experience; therefore, the ways of doing things are always in line with those who inhabit and write, with their times. Dissident bodies breaking into the very masculine and white publishing world. Questioning the bodies of hegemonic feminism that inhabit editorial spaces. "Being a fat lesbian and inhabiting sanitized publishing spaces is a rupture and a constant difficulty."[10]

Given that, this project arises from the bowels, from the sharing of experiences, from doing it in workshops, from coming together among women, lesbians, and racialized comrades to create small fissures within the feminist movement, publishing, and the heteropatriarchal colonial capitalist world. The publishing practices are small-scale, handmade, and always in collaboration with what is available. Books have their pulse, their rhythm, and their own vitality. Each one is based on the relationship built with the person who writes it, there is a process of inhabiting the publication that begins from the affectivities and the complicity-conspiracies between colleagues. Furthermore, Contreras

---

9 Canal Freak, "Editoriales independientes en La Furia del Libro" (January 6, 2020). http://canalfreak.net/especial-01-editoriales-independientes-en-la-furia-del-libro

10 Canal Freak, 2020.

conducts writing workshops with dissident bodies where experience is shared through words. The body of texts published by the publisher configures a network of dissident dialogue which questions the racist and colonial heteropatriarchy.

Another important project is that of Bicha Trava Publishing, which is an artistic space in Rio Cuarto, Córdoba, Argentina. For six years they have been editing, disseminating, and searching out trans, *travestis*, non-binary, whores, homos, racialized people, indies, gypsies, blacks, lesbians, and women authors. In their own words:

> A transvestite-trans publisher from South America, Córdoba, and cardboard. Maybe it can be difficult to understand for all those who think and associate the trans-*travesti* with certain and specific places. In this publishing world full of breeders, workers and hypocrites, our *travesti* being jumps for joy listening to our own and others' voices and screams. Accompany the work of a publisher that seeks cohesion between the cardboard, the trans, the recycling, the anti-colonialism with the fight against the hypocrites, the hatred and the crap from the academy.[11] (2021, online)

This project appears in 2015 as a space of "collective creation and publication of recycle, self-managed and anti-authoritarian". They do not edit cis heterosexual men, denouncing this would be a "political act of systemic reproduction."[12]

These experiences establish ideas that allow me to think of the feminist publication as a political space which is part of the experience, where the publication has a body and is continually put forward to question a system of death and the relationships that it produces and reproduces. The feminist edition opens the door to imagine ourselves in doing, inhabiting another way because the words that it decides to circulate are from a collective and personal experience which continues to point out the injustices and practices of death, while generating others and circulating narratives and collective imaginations that build other fields of the possible, where social transformation does not make invisible the heteropatriarchy that continues to consume many movements and spaces on the left. Because the bodies placed

---

11   La Bicha Trava, https://labichatrava.wordpress.com/ (accessed 2021).

12   La Bicha Trava.

there in the experience narrate other stories where the notion of success and the protagonist is diluted into an echo of many voices telling a story—it is time we pay attention to them in order to destabilize the heteropatriarchal siege of publishing and of a world that wants to close but which we continually kick and hit to keep it open, always breaking that crack open a little more, enabling us to inhabit better futures today.

I always have questions I want to keep open because they are also part of the path. I would like to close with all those question marks that lead me to continue thinking about the issue. I want to resonate more in the open questions than in the answers given, and with them the path is opened for us to continue thinking, building, and transforming as a collective. So here they are. What is, then, publishing in a heteropatriarchal, colonial-racist, and capitalist system? What is our role? What openings, what closures, are we enabling, empowering? What is our role in that? Are there leaks? What are they? What spaces do we have, how do we create them and most importantly, how do we sustain them?

Links to Publishing Projects Mentioned in this Essay

- FEA
  Facebook   https://www.facebook.com/FEAEDITORIAL/
  Instagram   https://www.instagram.com/feaeditorial/

- Ediciones la social
  Website   https://edicioneslasocial.wordpress.com/
  Instagram   https://www.instagram.com/edicioneslasocial

- Kalicabra
  Facebook   https://www.facebook.com/kalicabra/

- Fusilemos la noche
  Instagram   https://www.instagram.com/fusilemoslanoche.editorial
  Website   https://fusilemoslanoche.wordpress.com/

- La Reci
  Facebook   https://www.facebook.com/LaReci.libros/
  Instagram   https://www.instagram.com/larecitaller

- Pensaré Cartoneras

Website   https://pensarecartoneras.wordpress.com/
Facebook   https://www.facebook.com/pensarecartonera/

- Alcohol y Fotocopias
Website   http://alcoholyfotocopiasediciones.blogspot.com/
Facebook   https://m.facebook.com/profile.php?id=100063070757009
Instagram https://www.instagram.com/alcoholyfotocopias

- Bombas para Desayunar
Blog   http://bombasparadesayunar.blogspot.com/p/bpd-zines.html
Website   https://bombasparadesayunar.bigcartel.com/
Facebook   https://www.facebook.com/bombasparadesayunar/

- La Bicha Trava
Instagram https://www.instagram.com/labichatrava

Independent Publishers of the Editorial Market of the City of Belo Horizonte, Brazil

Terezinha de Fátima Carvalho de Souza

Introduction

The commercialization of knowledge, as said by Peter Burke,[1] is not something new and as an example he mentioned the British Copyright Act of 1709 which, in its preamble, aimed "to encourage men of culture to write useful books." For Burke that meant the novel was not part of the knowledge universe. The creation of the Royal Society in London brought the intention of putting in contact not only those who exercised intellectual activities, but also merchants and travelers who had access to knowledge produced in various cities in Europe, already a combination of knowledge creation and commerce, so characteristic of modern science.

In the commercialization process, the figure of the editor is fixed in the 1830s who, according to Roger Chartier's report,[2] "...is a profession of intellectual and commercial nature that aims to search for texts, to find authors, link them to the publisher, control the process that goes from printing the work to its distribution." Chartier also recalls that, between the 16th and 18th centuries, the publisher was known as "bookseller-publisher" or "graphic-editor," considering that it was in the bookstore that the editorial activity was organized. But the publisher could own his own printer or pass the printing activity to another.

---

1   Peter Burke, Uma história social do conhecimento, (Rio de Janeiro: Jorge Zahar Editor, 2003).

2   Roger Chartier, A aventura do livro: do leitor ao navegador (São Paulo: UNESP, 2009), 50.

Over the years, editors emerged who had a great passion for their activity, mainly composed of professionals who recognized editors as prestigious intellectuals. In the words of Nuno Medeiros,[3] an editor was a mix between a man of letters and a businessman. Due to this characteristic, many publishers had their own bookstores that offered a space for authors and readers to meet and carry out exchanges of great value; this value was considered, within the production and commercialization process, more important than just the financial result.

Medeiros comments:

> Despite the differences in the discursive framework that gives rise to it (from the scientific to the professional), the profusion of adjectives, occasionally attributed to specific editors such as antonomasia, suggests a procedural reading: from its autonomy at the dawn of the 19th century vis-à-vis other actors in the world of the book, the editor expanded and complexified his attributions palette, diversifying a profile whose typification became less obvious. From holder of technical knowledge to industrial manager, from "orchestra-man" to "prospector" of talents [Bassy 1991], from commercial producer of a cultural good to hierarch of the intellect. Progressively away from the dilettante archetype, the craft will organize itself professionally and separate attributions traditionally united in a single agent, opening doors to the consolidation of the idea of publishing house and authorizing the decline of individuality as a reference for the activity.[4]

Over the last few decades, publishing has gone through many changes and large media conglomerates have dominated the publishing market, bringing a vision only of "business." With this vision, the focus shifts to those projects that will bring the best financial results and in the shortest amount of time. With the strength of capital, these groups come to exercise hegemonic control over the market.

Independent media seek to make room for critical thinking, since the vast majority of corporate media are dominated by hegemonic thinking, in the Gramscian conception.

---

3   Simpósio Internacional "Por uma lei da bibliodiversidade" (São Paulo: Instituto de estudos Avançados da USP, October, 13-15 2021).

4   Nuno Medeiros, Notas sobre o mundo social do livro: a construção do editor e da edição," Revista Angolana de Sociologia, 9, 2012, 34. https://doi.org/10.4000/ras.412.

Hegemony is perceived as the possibility that a dominant group can reveal itself as a bearer of general interest and thus be recognized, unlike domination which needs a process of coercion to assert itself; therefore, hegemony gains "a qualitatively different status" as mentioned by Vadell.[5] And this is also felt in the publishing market, where corporate publishers have taken over.

During the period of dictatorship in Brazil (1964-1985), the so-called alternative media emerged, formed mainly by newspapers and magazines, seeking exactly to face the great censorship introduced in the country that dominated the corporate media and prevented information from reaching the public.[6] This was only possible through an "independent" distribution.

According to José de Souza Muniz Jr.,[7] the expression independent journalism brought resonances to the book world "when the editor conceives his activity as free from the interference of pressure groups interested in the dissemination of certain titles, areas or emphasis on the detriment of others."

Also, according to Muniz Jr., between the end of the 2000s and the beginning of the 2010s, book fairs emerged that gave visibility to publishing projects recognized as "independent." Many editors use book fairs to publicize their projects, along with their social networks and websites.

The website Editoras de Livros[8] features 450 publishers known as commercial. The commercial publisher is characterized as one that takes care of the production, dissemination, distribution, and sale of books, differentiating itself from service-providing publishers that sell the book production to authors and do not distribute them in bookstores. On the Editoras de Livros website, 24 commercial publishers were identified in Belo Horizonte, capital of the State of Minas Gerais. However, the publishing market in Belo Horizonte is larger. Independent

---

5   J. Vadell, "O papel dos think tanks na construção da hegemonia neoliberal," in *Instituições internacionais: Segurança, comércio e integração*, edited by Paulo Luiz Esteves (Belo Horizonte: PUCMINAS, 2003), 277.

6   Maria Lúcia Becker, "Mídia alternativa: Antiempresarial, antiindustrial, anticapitalista?" in *Recortes da mídia alternativa: Histórias & memórias da comunicação no Brasil*, edited by Karina Janz Woitowicz (Ponta Grossa: Ed. UEPG, 2009).

7   José de Souza Muniz Jr., *Girafas e bonsais: Editores "independentes" na Argentina e no Brasil (1991-2015)* (dissertation, Universidade de São Paulo, 2016), 270.

8   www.editorasdelivros.com.br.

publishers, those that give voice to themes others than those of hegemonic thought, feature productions by independent authors, and often use the practice of crowdfunding. These publishers are often looking for other means of advertising since the major media outlets do not embrace them.

As Iara Augusta da Silva[9] reaffirms, the world and the Brazilian publishing market has been undergoing transformations along with those of contemporary capitalist society. As in other economic sectors, the publishing market is experiencing an accelerated process of mergers and acquisitions and it is increasingly possible to see a smaller number of companies monopolizing the market.

The Liga Brasileira de Editoras (LIBRE) is a network of independent publishers that work cooperatively to strengthen their businesses, the publishing market, and bibliodiversity. LIBRE is an association of public interest; it is non-profit, non-political party affiliated, and free and independent from public and governmental agencies. It was established on August 1st, 2002. It sets as its mission "to preserve bibliodiversity in the Brazilian publishing market by strengthening independent publishing as business and is constituted as a network of collaborative editors aiming for reflection and taking action towards the expansion of the readership, the strengthening of independent publishing companies, and the creation of public policies favoring books and the act of reading."[10]

Between October 13 and 15, 2021, the "International Symposium for Bibliodiversity Law" was held by the Institute of Advanced Studies of the University of São Paulo. This event was attended by Brazilian and French speakers. When celebrating the 40 years of the so called "Lang Law" or "Law for Fixed Prices" in France, the theme was debated by representatives who defend the enactment of this law by Brazilian Congress, as well as by professors and representatives from publishers and publisher associations, including independent ones. Some of the issues discussed are notable, such as the relevance of cultural diversity promoted by independent publishers and the need for price regulation of new books. Another pointed issue was that large

---

9   Iara Augusta da Silva, "A conformação do mercado editorial brasileiro a partir das últimas décadas do século XX e nos anos iniciais do século XXI: O caso do Grupo Abril," *Revista HISTEDBR On-line*, 60, 2014, 78-94. https://periodicos.sbu.unicamp.br/ojs/index.php/histedbr/article/view/8640549/8108

10 www.libre.org.br

hypermarkets require commercial publishers to offer high discounts on the cover price and, therefore, place books at a much lower price than bookstores. To meet this requirement, publishers raise their prices and bookstores cannot compete.

Another issue addressed was the cost of sending copies. There is a movement in Brazil to totally privatize the postal service. This cost is still regulated by the State and in a country with continental dimensions, this is a matter of relevance. Once this service is completely privatized, cost control will be impossible.

Despite the difficulties encountered, especially in this long period of the COVID-19 pandemic, independent publishers continue to struggle to be present in the publishing market.

The publishers presented below participated in the 12th Textura Fair, held in Belo Horizonte, in January 2020, before the beginning of the social isolation due to the COVID-19 pandemic. This fair is organized by the independent publisher "Impressões de Minas," which is also responsible for holding the Urucum fairs (graphic arts and artist books) and the Curupira Fair (visual arts and children's publications).

Methodology

Through the Textura Fair page on Facebook, 14 publishers were identified, all of whom participated in the fair as well featured information on their social media. Initially, a survey of information about each of them was carried out; it appears at the end of this chapter.

After this survey, an email was sent to the editors and we received responses from five of them. An interview was then conducted with each one virtually, in order to understand their processes for selecting, producing, distributing, and advertising their products.

An interview was also carried out with the editor responsible for organizing the Textura Fair, our initial source of information.

Analysis and Results

We grouped the results from the interviews based on four research topics: selection, production, distribution, and dissemination. Not everyone answered all the questions and therefore, the number of considerations on each topic varies.

Selection

"Created in 2019, this publisher has a feminist editorial approach that exclusively puts out books written by women, having nine books printed and more in production. Texts goes through an editorial board and the general editor. This council is composed of professional women of letters and/or researchers from different areas of knowledge. Some names are permanent, others are temporary collaborators—as was the case with the council formed specifically for the selection of texts from an open call made in January 2020."

"The groundbreaking moment for this publisher came from the experience of translating a book from French to Portuguese. The first book could only be published after the publisher's registration with the MEI,[11] since before that it was impossible to pay the copyright in euros. There was a stoppage after this publication and an effective resumption of activities in 2017, with a publication by the publisher and two more children's texts. This publisher receives originals for evaluation through contacts from the authors themselves."

"It's a peculiar process. No notices or calls for publications are made. Authors usually look for this publisher. So, initially, research is made about the author."

"An editorial team evaluates the incoming texts, analyzing whether they fit the catalogue, with a criterion model defined by the publisher's policy and culture. They do not have open public calls for original work. Some originals are the result of prospecting and others arrive from our sources or through the website, Instagram, and other contact channels. A contract is made in which most of the time 10% of copyright is paid. Some projects receive public funding from universities, CEFETs[12], and schools."

"Currently, the editor makes the editorial choices for the surveys that are carried out. In addition, works that arrive through agencies or agents are analyzed. The choice of originals has been done in this way, as the call for originals that had been carried out in recent years is currently suspended."

---

11   MEI stands for Individual Micro-entrepreneur, that is, a self-employed professional. When you register as a micro-entrepreneur, you have the facilities to open a bank account, apply for loans, and issue invoices, in addition to having the obligations and rights of a legal entity. See www.sebrae.com.br

12   Editors' note: CEFET stands for Federal Center for Technological Education and offer a technology-focused curriculum for high school, vocational, and university-level students.

Regarding the selection processes, it was possible to observe that, perhaps because they are small publishers, there is no standardization of actions for prospecting originals. The publisher itself often prospects these originals in different ways.

Production

"The production is completely done by women and, for each project, a team of freelancers is assembled. All projects are coordinated by the publisher: layout, proofreading, cover, graphic design, and evaluating the product. The commercial and financial part is handled by another professional."

"Production becomes a slower process, since the publisher has to bear all the costs, as the contracts are not a provision of services. Small publishers take more risks, it's bibliodiversity. Each one has its own way and they are all different."

"Currently, independent authors hire the work of the publisher and the marketing is done by the author themself. Few titles are fully produced by the publisher. Another stranglehold is the price of paper. In Brazil, a single company has monopoly on paper production, thus the price is defined by this industry. In one year, the price was raised four times. Strong state intervention would be needed to end this monopoly and subsidize small businesses."

"In general, the production takes place as in any other publisher, respecting all editorial processes: text editing, proofreading, preparation, layout, thinking about the graphic design and cover, as well as the best ways to disseminate the work itself. Everything is done by the two partners of the publisher along with freelancers. Authors follow along nearly every process until the book is finished."

Given the difficulties inherent to the businesses of small publishers, the existence of fixed production teams in the publishers was not verified. They work with teams of temporary freelance staff.

Distribution

"Most sales are made through the publisher's online store. There is great interest in increasing the distribution of books, which is one of the biggest challenges for small publishers. Distributors and bookstores charge for resale between 45-60% of the cover price. So far, they have direct partnerships with bookstores and women entrepreneurs in the cities of São Paulo, Belo Horizonte, Montes Claros, Rio de Janeiro, and Salvador."

"Distribution is more complicated than production. The business model used by bookstores is by consignment and they demand discounts of 40-50% of the cover price."

"Distribution in bookstores is difficult because, in addition to having to offer a discount of up to 50%, for the book to be displayed it is necessary to pay an advance. Small publishers cannot compete. Due to short runs, it is only possible to offer a discount of at most 30% to be able to pay the production cost. Controlling sales and making financial arrangements with bookstores is quite complicated. With distributors it is not much different, it is even more difficult to control the books in their stocks. Both bookstores and distributors use the consignment system. Thus, the publisher has to bear the entire cost of production and will only recover its investment after the sale."

"Done by three distributors and about 45 bookstores nationwide, mainly in the capitals."

"Distribution takes place through bookstores and distributors with which the publisher works constantly. In addition, there is a representative who acts as an intermediary with some customers, bookstores, and distributors, other actions are taken care of by the two partners."

It was possible to observe that those publishers that have been in the market for a longer time and have greater economic and financial stability are able to better deal with the demands of distributors and bookstores. The others try to distribute and sell by themselves through e-commerce.

Advertising

"The fairs are very important, not because of their sales, but because of their proximity to the public, authors, and editorial production professionals, such as illustrators. The exchange between editors is also interesting. In addition to the fairs, there is a website for dissemination and social networks, such as Instagram."

"The dissemination is done through social networks, the publisher does not have a mailing list yet. Fairs are also used for publicity, as there is rarely a profit from sales. There is very strong competition with outlet sellers from big bookstores, who pass to sellers for very low prices and small publishers cannot compete. Participating in local fairs is a little more viable because participation costs are lower. To recover the investment, it would be necessary to sell at least 70 copies, which is very difficult to happen at a fair."

"Today social networks are fundamental, they have been the main source of contact with the public, mainly Instagram and Facebook. Book fairs are also very important. The publisher is responsible for holding three fairs: a general one, focused on diversity, another focused on artists and publishers that publish artists' books, and another focused on children's literature."

All interviewed publishers presented social media and fairs as the main forms of advertising, but highlighted the great difficulties faced by small businesses, recognized here as independent, in relation to the high costs of publicity.

In the words of the organizer of the Textura Fair, the fairs are all produced in a completely independent process. They are popular, democratic spaces that facilitate research, contacts, and discussions and strengthen the richness of bibliodiversity. At the fair there is the author, the editor, the illustrator, and the general public, all in the same space exchanging ideas about the book's universe—from the production stage all the way up to commercialization. In addition, fairs are an opportunity for those independent authors and small publishers who are not part of a catalog to get into bookstores.

Conclusion

It is interesting to mention that two of the interviewees manifested themselves in relation to the Fixed Price Law, with opposite positions. One of them considers for the small publisher it will make no difference, maintaining an uneven competitive system. As for the other editor, he considers that the law is very necessary, decreeing the sale price of the book to the final consumer cannot be set below 90% of the cover price decided by the publisher, during the 12-month period, counting from the release date.[13] The idea is to have a fairer mar-

---

13 Projeto de Lei do Senado n° 49, de 2015 ("Lei José Xavier Cortez"). https://www25.senado.leg.br/web/atividade/materias/-/materia/119760 Editors' note: This bill was originally proposed in its current form in 2015, shelved for several years, revived and renamed in honor of José Xavier Cortez, a bookseller and publisher, who championed the issue. As of 2024, the bill is in committee with the Brazilian Senate.

ket for the entire sector, including readers and publishers, preventing high discounts that cause a disparity mainly between the book market and the end consumer. When the market discounts prices, it makes variety and bibliodiversity impossible. Price maintenance for a period of 12 months after release covers exactly the period when the book sells the most. It is necessary to ensure a value that everyone can work with, avoiding the "economic terrorism" practiced by large multinational corporations that weaken book wealth in every sense and scale.

Another interesting aspect that we can observe is that independent editors represent a way of resistance and in this matter, they remind us of the beginning of the publishing market, when editors had, above all else, a great passion for the universe of letters, just like the one we find in independent editors today, fiercely determined to maintain bibliodiversity.

Bibliography

Becker, Maria Lúcia. "Mídia alternativa: Antiempresarial, anti-industrial, anti-capitalista?" in *Recortes da mídia alternativa: Histórias & memórias da comunicação no Brasil*, edited by Karina Janz Woitowicz. Ponta Grossa: Ed. UEPG, 2009. 273-286.

Burke, Peter. *Uma história social do conhecimento*. Rio de Janeiro: Jorge Zahar Editor, 2003.

Chartier, Roger. *A aventura do livro: Do leitor ao navegador*. São Paulo: UNESP, 2009.

Medeiros, Nuno. "Notas sobre o mundo social do livro: A construção do editor e da edição." *Revista Angolana de Sociologia*, 9, 2012, 33-48. https://doi.org/10.4000/ras.412

Muniz Jr., José de Souza. *Girafas e bonsais: Editores "independentes" na Argentina e no Brasil (1991-2015)*. Dissertation, Universidade de São Paulo, 2016.

Silva, Iara Augusta da. "A conformação do mercado editorial brasileiro a partir das últimas décadas do século XX e nos anos iniciais do século XXI: O caso do Grupo Abril." *Revista HISTEDBR On-line*, n. 60, 2014, 78-94. https://periodicos.sbu.unicamp.br/ojs/index.php/histedbr/article/view/8640549/8108

Vadell, J. "O papel dos think tanks na construção da hegemonia neoliberal," in *Instituições internacionais: Segurança, comércio e integração.*, by Paulo Luiz Esteves. Belo Horizonte: PUCMINAS, 2003. 376-401.

List of Publishers Consulted

- Aletria Editora
  aletria.com.br

- Ateliê de Livros Malcriados
  Facebook @livrosmalcriados
  Instagram @atelie_livrosmalcriados

- Cas'a Edições
  casaedicoes.com

- Caos & Letras
  caoseletras.com

- Editora Luas
  editoraluas.com.br

- Editora Moinhos
  editoramoinhos.com.br

- Editora Venas Abiertas
  venasabiertas.com.br

- EIS Editora
  eiseditora.com.br

- Francesinha Editora
  editorafrancesinha.com.br

- Impressões de Minas
  impressoesdeminas.com.br

- Páginas Editora
  Instagram @paginaseditora

- PHONTE88
  phonte.hotglue.me

- Relicário Edições
  relicarioedicoes.com

- SQN Biblioteca
  sqnbiblioteca.com.br

The Power of Social and Cultural Capital
Investing in 21st Century Learners Through Access to Latin American Indigenous Works

Kathia Salomé Ibacache Oliva

Introduction

This chapter aims to kindle a conversation about the benefits of building a collection that considers Indigenous authors among academic librarians with collection development responsibilities. I will argue that building social and cultural capital is relevant not only for collection development practices but also to enhance 21st century learners. The chapter follows a narrative backed by scholarly sources and emphasizes the importance of academic libraries to support learners by facilitating access to works produced or written by underrepresented authors. In addition, the chapter includes insights from interviews with three small book publishers and vendors from Latin America who provide works by Indigenous authors. The interviewees answered the following two questions: 1) What challenges do you see to access the university libraries market? 2) What suggestions do you have for university libraries that would like to create a formal business relationship with small publishers and book vendors of underrepresented authors and literature?

The Power of Social Capital

What do we understand by having social capital? The concept of social capital has undergone several realignments throughout its sociological conception. For example, Karl Marx, who conceptualized "capital" in the 19th century, believed capitalists had an exploitative relationship with the proletariat.[1] Nonetheless, some scholars see social capital as an investment in social networks with the expectation of a profit.[2] Professor of political theory, James Farr, discusses the conceptual history of social capital and reaffirms that this capital has been defined differently by scholars. Moreover, Farr identified people from different fields to have utilized this concept, such as Pierre Bourdieu, the economist Glen Loury, the social psychologist John R. Seeley, and the educator Lyda J. Hanifan.[3] Hanifan used this concept in his piece "A Story of Achievement" in 1916 and his book "The Community Center" in 1920.[4]

John Dewey, another educator, and philosopher referred to social capital in four of his publications during the early 1900s.[5] During his remarks at the National Negro Conference in 1909, Dewey stated that an inferior race does not exist; society is responsible for providing an environment that would enhance individuals' capital, regardless of their race, and that failure to do so would tarnish social capital.[6] However, it was Bourdieu who expanded on the notion of social capital.[7] For Bourdieu, the amount of social capital is attached to the "size of the network of connections," and the profits or benefits a person acquires depends on the amount of economic and cultural capital the members of that network possess.[8]

Explaining Bourdieu's theorization, sociologist Alejandro Portes notes that social networks must be nurtured to be beneficial to a group and that there are two aspects in Bourdieu's social capital definition that

---

1 Nan Lin, "Building a Network Theory of Social Capital," *Connections* 22, no. 1 (1999): 28-30.

2 Ibid., 31, 39.

3 James Farr, "Social Capital: A Conceptual History." *Political Theory* 32, no. 1 (2004): 7. Doi:10.1177/0090591703254978.

4 Ibid., 11.

5 Ibid., 17.

6 "Proceeding of the National Negro Conference," (New York, May 31 and June 1st 1909): 71-2, accessed September 7, 2021, http://moses.law.umn.edu/darrow/documents/Proceedings%20of%20the%20National%20Negro%20Conference%201909_%20New%20York_%20May%2031%20and%20June_1.pdf.

7 Pierre Bourdieu's chapter "The Forms of Capital" expands on the concept of cultural and social capital. Bourdieu, "The Forms of Capital," in *Handbook of Theory of Research for the Sociology of Education*, ed. J.E. Richardson, trans. Richard Nice (Westport, CT: Greenwood Press, 1986), 46–51. See also Alejandro Portes "Social Capital: Its Origins and Applications in Modern Sociology," *Annual Review of Sociology* vol. 24 (1998): 3.

8 Bourdieu, "The Forms of Capital," 21.

are relevant. First, people have access to resources available through their social relationships; second, these resources vary in amount and quality.[9] Portes also mentions Loury, who in the late 1970s examined "racial income inequality" concerning parental economic success and social relationships as a variable for a person's achievement.[10] Loury states,

> The merit notion, that in a free society each individual will rise to the level justified by his or her competence, conflicts with the observation that no one travels that road entirely alone. The social content within which individual maturation occurs strongly conditions what otherwise equally competent individuals can achieve. This implies that absolute equality of opportunity, where an individual's chance to succeed depends only on his or her innate capabilities, is an ideal that cannot be achieved...[11]

Similarly, sociologist James Samuel Coleman referring to the effect of social capital within the family and the community in the creation of human capital provides a function-based definition of social capital, highlighting that social structures are a part of the equation and that social capital is "productive" facilitating results that would not be possible without it.[12] In other words, even when a person has merit, social context is needed for better achievement. Therefore, networks are essential to building social capital.

In the case of collection development of Latin American Indigenous languages materials, I consider social capital based on fruitful inter-regional relationships among a group of individuals who gain different benefits through cooperation. I borrow Farr's term "cooperative association" to reason that without the collaboration of this network of individuals (subject specialists, acquisitions personnel, and book vendors and distributors of works written by minority authors,) it would be onerous to offer access to works by Indigenous authors to

---

9   Alejandro Portes, "Social Capital: Its Origins and Applications in Modern Sociology," *Annual Review* 24 (1998): 3-4.

10 Ibid., 4; see also Glenn C. Loury, "A Dynamic Theory of Racial Income Differences," In *Women, Minorities, and Employment Discrimination*," Ed. P.A. Wallace and A. La Mond, (Lexington Books, Lexington, MA 1977), 155.

11 Loury, 176.

12 James Coleman S., "Social Capital and the Creation of Human Capital," *The American Journal of Sociology* 94, no. 1988 (1988): S98. See also Portes, 6.

members of a university.[13] Loury's postulation that "no one travels that road entirely alone," stated above, makes sense at the academic and achievement level. Faculty and graduate students rely on the libraries to access the literature needed for their research or courses. Similarly, students depend on their professors and teaching assistants to understand topics covered in class; students may also expect help from the libraries accessing all types of materials. Last, the libraries depend on publishers, vendors, and distributors to provide access to print and electronic sources.

Portes asserts that the empirical literature considers social capital with the benefits accrued by belonging to a social network or other social structure.[14] If one contends that for developing inclusive collections, our social network is built with inter-regional agents, this cooperative association may facilitate access to marginalized literature and films that otherwise would be absent from collegiate collections. In Portes's words, "to possess social capital, a person must be related to others, and it is those others, not himself, who are the actual source of his or her advantage."[15]

The Power of Cultural Capital

Similar to social capital, cultural capital presupposes a particular type of profit. Bourdieu formulated the term when he examined the role of the educational system in the reproduction and distribution of cultural capital in his chapter "Cultural Reproduction and Social Reproduction" in 1973.[16] Bourdieu deployed the cultural capital theory to explain children's uneven school achievement when belonging to different social classes.[17] For Bourdieu, cultural capital has three forms: the embodied state, the objectified state, and the institutionalized state.[18] The embodied state represents the symbolic aspect of this capital,

---

13 Farr, 8, 19, 24, 27.

14 Portes, 6.

15 Ibid., 7.

16 Bourdieu, "Cultural Reproduction and Social reproduction" in *Knowledge, Education, and Cultural Change* ed. Richard Brown (Routledge Library Editions), 1973.

17 "The Forms of Capital," 17; Annick Prieur and Mike Savage, "Emerging Forms of Cultural Capital," *European Societies* 15, no. 2 (2013): 247. DOI: 10.1080/14616696.2012.748930.

18 Ibid.

such as knowledge, mannerism, and language.[19] The objectified state represents materials or cultural goods such as clothing, paintings, instruments, machines, and most relevant to this chapter, books, etc.[20] The institutionalized state refers to a person's credentials such as college degree and institutional affiliation.[21]

However, sociologists wonder whether Bourdieu's theorization of cultural capital may still be applied today.[22] Especially in the 21st century, when access to information via electronic devices, for example, has shifted the dynamics of knowledge and skill acquisition. Annick Prieur and Mike Savage note that technological and social changes as seen in the advent of personal computers and student activism are some of the events that signal significant differences between the time Bourdieu associated cultural capital with highbrow culture and current times.[23] Nonetheless, Sociologist Nicki Lisa Cole states that cultural capital in an objectified state represents a person's economic class, adding that social roles are also utilized to measure cultural capital.[24] For Cole, every person has cultural capital, but the cultural capital of the elite is different from the cultural capital of other social groups, and this distinction is relevant significantly when society does not value all types of cultural capital equally.[25]

At the university level, libraries serve all students and members of the academic institution, regardless of social rank. Nonetheless, this service becomes crucial to level up access to resources and information for those with less economic capital and affected by unequal distribution of goods and services. Suppose Bourdieu perceived that cultural capital accentuated social divisions and inequality; in that case, when it comes to information, university libraries provide access to a wide variety of resources and information, lessening this inequality.

---

19 Nicki Lisa Cole, "What Is Cultural Capital? Do I Have It?" ThoughtCo., Accessed September 9, 2021, https://www.thoughtco.com/whatis-cultural-capital-do-i-have-it-3026374.

20 "The Forms of Capital," 17.

21 Ibid., 20.

22 Annick Prieur and Mike Savage.

23 Ibid., 249.

24 Cole.

25 Ibid.

Bourdieu declares that capital has the "capacity to produce profits."[26] If we consider the objectified state of cultural capital as theorized by Bourdieu, this capital may translate into better educational opportunities and performance. Whether lacking cultural capital leads to social inequality, the libraries may acquire the materials needed to fill in an information resource gap. For example, if a student in economic need is working on a course-related research paper, a dissertation, or an honor thesis covering indigeneity, the university libraries' support may lead to better student performance and course preparation, better grades, and more knowledge. In other words, the libraries provide access to resources that may help students do well at school and in other areas of their life.

However, to acquire materials, university libraries must have a network of connections that will supply such materials, especially those of underrepresented literature, and building this network might be challenging. There is the time investment needed to find vendors in the Americas that provide the work of Indigenous authors, budget, and language barrier. Moreover, even when a purchasing relationship is made, issues may arise involving the purchasing transaction itself. Regardless, by facilitating access to books written by Indigenous authors, university libraries are enhancing the cultural capital of students and the libraries themselves.

When university libraries invest in strengthening relationships with small book publishers and book distributors, more opportunities will emerge to provide books from underrepresented authors and thus advance the knowledge attainment opportunities for 21st century learners. Citing Bourdieu, Cole mentions "that cultural capital exists in a system of exchange with economic and social capital," which is why it is vital developing purchasing relationships with book and film vendors who carry the work of Indigenous writers or Indigenous-related works that only specific publishers and vendors offer.

Building Indigenous Collections

Academic libraries in the United States build their collections through a variety of purchasing methods: approval plans (contract-based with book vendors), standing orders (books from series), firm orders (direct

---

26   Ibid., 15.

requests from users), suggest a title for purchase programs, or by ProQuest approval. Similar purchasing methods apply when building DEI collections. The American Library Association (ALA) advises in "content criteria" and general criteria for school library selection to consider works that represent diverse points of view and those that "provide a global perspective" with authors from different cultures.[27] Similarly, ALA notes that collection development should include content that embodies "marginalized and underrepresented groups."[28]

Some university libraries in the United States are implementing changes to diversify collections concerning Indigenous collections. To illustrate, the University of Denver Libraries' Collection Diversification Task Force found five strategies to diversify collections, emphasizing the Cheyenne and Arapaho tribes. The first two strategies update approval plans to include GOBI and small publishers of Native American works. The third strategy creates a local thesaurus representing all Native American tribes. The fourth strategy compares the University of Denver collections to other collections from the area to establish gaps and overlaps. The last strategy entails outreach to the local Cheyenne and Arapaho communities to gather feedback.[29]

Similarly, the University of Colorado Boulder (CU Boulder) Libraries are also doing intentional work to create a Latin American Indigenous languages and cultures collection. CU Boulder seeks to highlight the literary work of Indigenous authors, including film productions where indigeneity, cosmovision, and other Andean themes from an Indigenous perspective are relevant. In the article "Forgotten Hispano-American Literature: Representation of Hispano-American Presses in Academic Libraries," I refer to the literary value of works such as *Paloma Torcaza*, by Sócrates Zuzunaga Huaita, a winner of the Primer Premio of Literature Quechua, and *Hilando en la Memoria*, a book of poems by 14 Mapuche women written in Mapudungun language with Spanish

---

27 American Library Association. "Selection Criteria," (2018), accessed September 8, 2021, www.ala.org/tools/challengesupport/selectionpolicytoolkit/criteria.

28 American Library Association. "Diverse Collections: An Interpretation of the Library Bill of Rights," accessed September 9, 2021, https://www-ala-org.colorado.idm.oclc.org/advocacy/intfreedom/librarybill/interpretations/diversecollections.

29 Jennifer Martin, "New Research in Collection Management," ALA Annual Conference News, (August 2019), accessed September 9, 2021, https://alcts.ala.org/news/2019/new-research-in-collection-management-alaac19/.

translation. These two books are a small example of valued literature published in regional publisher houses.[30]

In addition, some universities have created digital libraries focused on research and propagation, the Universidad Autónoma de México created the "Biblioteca Digital de la Medicina Tradicional Mexicana," including bilingual (Indigenous and Spanish language) information about regional plants used by Indigenous peoples for medicinal purposes, and traditional medicine used by Indigenous people in Mexico.[31] In addition, the University of Texas Libraries and the University of Texas at Austin's College of Liberal Arts supported "The Archive of the Indigenous Languages of Latin America," a digital language archive containing dictionaries, ethnographies, field notes, and recordings—audio and video—of chants, oratory, narratives, songs, and conversations.[32] These initiatives attest to the work done by some universities in building Indigenous collections or an Indigenous presence in the library.

Establishing A Network

Doing business with large or mainstream book distributors and publishers may speed print book request processes, offer competitive prices, and facilitate communication, but large conglomerates do not usually offer marginalized literature and underrepresented authors. To access underrepresented literature, university libraries must consider small publishing houses, small booksellers, alternative publishing, and independent bookstores that may offer the works of underrepresented writers such as Indigenous authors. Brigitte Ouvry-Vial, comparing literary publishing in France by small and big publishers, notes a "cultural cost" when the production of multinational groups supersedes quality.[33] Moreover, she adds that small publishers maintain quality and low

---

30. Kathia Ibacache, Javier Alonso Muñoz-Diaz, Caitlin M. Berry, and Eric A. Vance, "Forgotten Hispano-American Literature: representation of Hispano-American Presses in Academic Libraries," *College & Research Libraries* 81, no. 6 (2020): 938-9, https://doi.org/10.5860/crl.81.6.928.

31. "Biblioteca Digital de la Medicina Tradicional Mexicana," Univeridad Nacional Autónoma de Mexico, accessed September 10, 2021, http://www.medicinatradicionalmexicana.unam.mx/index.html.

32. Llilas Benson Latin American Studies and Collections, the Department of Linguistics, and the Digital Library Services of the University Libraries at the University of Texas at Austin, "Archive of the Indigenous Languages of Latin America (AILLA), (2017), https://ailla.utexas.org/.

33. Brigitte Ouvry-Vial, "Small and Big Publishers in France: Is Literature a Rare Species?" *Publishing Research Quarterly* 19, no. 1 (2003): 33, https://doi.org/10.1007/s12109-003-0021-7.

cost, providing a space for international writers and new authors.[34] Ouvry-Vial's reference to "cultural cost" may imply that if librarians do not seek small, independent, and non-profit presses or publishers that offer diverse, provocative, marginal, and experimental works, then underrepresented literature and films might not reach constituents.

Therefore, the work of librarians with collection development responsibilities must be intentional when it comes to building inclusive collections. Another helpful practice is the communication among subject librarians and different personnel from acquisitions, who will also be a part of this network or cooperative association. Will a formal understanding with the vendor be made via an approval plan or individual firm orders? The University of Colorado Boulder has made formal relationships with vendors from Latin America using Market Place, a clearinghouse platform that verifies vendors' information to secure payment via check through an invoice. Although doing business via firm orders may be more time-intensive, they provide an opportunity to establish a purchasing relationship when contracts-based approval plans are not feasible.

Finally, it is crucial to hear those who represent the book business of underrepresented literature. The feedback of people in the book business may enlighten librarians with collection development responsibilities, book vendors in general, and other agents from the book business. Through an email interview submitted in July 2021, a representative from Editorial Abya-Yala, F&G Editores, and Enhacore Books shared their views on two questions: 1) What challenges do you see to access the university libraries market? 2) What suggestions do you have for university libraries that would like to create a formal business relationship with small publishers and book vendors of underrepresented authors and literature?

To the question about challenges to access the university libraries market, the representatives noted that it is difficult for independent and regional book distributors to compete with large conglomerates that already have a relationship with educational institutions. The budget is also a challenge that may deter librarians from considering new "libreros" and publishing houses. In addition, these representatives cautioned against prioritizing electronic materials, which affect smaller

---

34   Ibid., 36-7.

publishing houses that offer underrepresented literature and usually produce print books. Taxes are another matter of concern when countries do not have a tax agreement with the United States, affecting the acquisition transaction with small businesses.

Regarding suggestions for university libraries that wish to create a formal business relationship with small publishers and book vendors of underrepresented authors and literature, representatives alluded to encouraging a relationship between large book distributors and smaller ones to provide universities with underrepresented, regional, and independent materials. This relationship is beneficial because large and small distributors have different focuses, and thus they may complement each other to serve the needs of libraries' collection development.

One representative also recommended forging relationships with "libreros;" by centralizing the acquisition of materials "libreros" could be the middleman between the regional publishing house or book distributor and the university library. However, this "librero" must be in a position of trust and have a regional presence to be aware of what is happening in the publishing landscape with publishing houses going out of business or vice versa. A compelling suggestion is to appreciate that the role of "libreros" goes beyond the purely economic act, inviting librarians to consider "libreros" as partners in collection development. Last, a representative suggested attending large-scale "Ferias del Libro" and those hosted at the regional level.

Conclusion

Inclusive collections that consider the works of Indigenous authors are beneficial for students, faculty, and the libraries as educational institutions that are a part of the revitalization of Indigenous languages and cultures. In this chapter, I argue that building social and cultural capital is relevant not only for collection development practices but also to enhance 21st century learners. University libraries would benefit from forging a symbiotic relationship, even if it is via a "librero," with small Latin American publishing houses and book vendors that promote underrepresented writers such as Indigenous authors. For university libraries with a network of connections that include small book publishers and book distributors of underrepresented authors, students and faculty have more opportunities to access authors' works absent in mainstream and prominent publishing platforms.

Although there are challenges to acquiring underrepresented literature, such as the literary output of Indigenous authors, representatives from Abya Yala, F&G Editores, and Enhacore Books have some suggestions:

1. Forging a relationship with "libreros" may facilitate a mutually beneficial relationship between large book distributors and small publishing houses, and book vendors of underrepresented materials.
2. It is consequential to acknowledge that publishers of underrepresented literature tend to publish in print format, and thus university libraries could be sensitive to this reality when allocating funds.
3. Visiting "Ferias Internacionales del Libro" is essential as they cover independent publishing houses.

However, librarians could also consider visiting specific countries and attending smaller regional "Feria del Libro" to familiarize themselves with the literary output of the region. Last, considering "libreros" as a member of the acquisition network of connections entails that this relationship goes beyond purely economic activity. This relationship guarantees that the materials university libraries purchase align with the institution's collection needs and the needs of the university members. Finally, through Farr's notion of "cooperative association," social capital will transcend to provide access to underrepresented materials that will nourish the cultural capital of those who access these materials, enhancing students' opportunities as 21st century learners.

Addendum

1. *What challenges do you see to access the university libraries market?*

Enhacore Books–Alejandro Herrera Prada

In some cases, the decades-long consolidation of suppliers of printed or electronic material diminishes the likelihood that new suppliers with different, independent, and/or regional material come to the attention of libraries. Budget cuts in libraries also reduce the possibility that librarians or curators can consider new titles from booksellers and publishers, since resources are prioritized for already established businesses. The prioritization of electronic material over printed material directly affects the possibility of supplying independent material from Colombia to these institutions because the underrepresented publishers, in general, always publish in printed format and with low print runs, so they would not be covered by the budgets for electronic books.

Abya Yala–Mónika Aranda

New challenges in teaching mean that university libraries must change to continue as centers of research and learning for the university community as well as for researchers. In this context, it is important to note that university libraries in the United States have automated their access, making it user-friendly and easy. Specialized collections makes it much easier for publishers to deliver material with different themes, both in physical and digital formats. They assume the costs of shipping, which for us are high and otherwise make the purchase difficult.

F&G Editores – Raúl Figueroa Sarti

The only thing that might be a barrier is tax registration, which is not always easy for a small business outside the United States.

2. *What suggestions do you have for university libraries that would like to create a formal business relationship with small publishers and book vendors of underrepresented authors and literature?*

Enhacore Books–Alejandro Herrera Prada

Experience has shown us that it is possible to maintain already established business with other large suppliers and to go through firm orders or other small agreements, allocating a portion of the acquisition budget to independent, regional, and underrepresented publishers. Usually the focus of the suppliers is different and they can complement each other, which can undoubtedly enrich the collection.

Personally, I would recommend that libraries interested in creating a formal relationship for the acquisition of this type of material do so through vendors with experience in this regard, based on:

- Since these are independent and regional publishers, they are usually very small and it is better for a vendor to coordinate the acquisition of material from a country or region rather than the library having a relationship with each of the publishers.

- These may be publishers that appear and disappear regularly. Working through a trusted vendor will allow the library to delegate the responsibility of keeping an eye on the developments of new publishers or self-publishing.

- Taking into account the above, I would recommend that the vendor the library works with have a presence in the region or country that it covers, and that the library can somehow verify that in fact that bookseller or distributor regularly travels to places where these underrepresented publications are available, which often do not even reach the capitals or major bookfairs of each country.

- Personally, I think that the role of the vendor should be allied to the development of the library collection, not merely as a commercial activity. The experience of the vendor or distributor is important so that the material supplied, even if it is independent or regional, is of value to the library collection. In this way, the supply of translations, co-editions, duplication or others that do not fit the profile of the library collection will be avoided. For example, things outside the client profile, such as translations, co-editions, and duplicates, can be avoided. This transcends the commercial work to focus on the selection and real coverage of the material that does not reach the capital cities.

Finally, I would recommend that librarians visit the region they wish to cover if possible, and I am not only referring to the large book fairs, which are doing important work in trying to cover a large part of the independent publishing sector (at least in Colombia), but also, depending on the focus, being able to visit other regional fairs such as the Medellín Book Festival (in the case of Colombia) or to arrange acquisition trips with vendors or distributors to facilitate an "in situ" perspective of what the region produces in this type of material.

Abya Yala–Mónika Aranda

The most important recommendation is to support small publishers by purchasing their books and not proliferate the distribution of digital versions without any kind of restrictions, which affects both the publisher and the author.

It must be taken into account that publishing a work often requires a great economic effort given the circumstances of Latin American countries in terms of the import of raw materials. The prices of books not only reflect these expenses, but also the effort and sacrifice of researching and shaping it into a publication. Recognizing this with the purchase of original books motivates researchers and publishers to continue with this laudable work toward the transmission of knowledge.

F&G Editores – Raúl Figueroa Sarti

Attend book fairs, as not all publishers can be at the biggest book fairs.

Contact

F&G Editores

Email	informacion@fygeditores.com
Website	fygeditores.com

Enhacore-Colombia Books

Email	info@colombiabooks.com info@enhacorebooks.com
Website	colombiabooks.com enhacorebooks.com

Editorial Abya Yala

Email	editorial@abyayala.org.ec ventas@abyayala.org.ec
Website	abyayala.org.ec

Artisanal Publishing

Malha Fina Cartonera
Trajectory and Itineraries of an Alternative Model for Publishing

Idalia Morejón Arnaiz, Pacelli Dias Alves de Sousa, and Chayenne Orru Mubarack

Translated by Lisa Gardinier

Mapping an Alternative Proposal: The Establishment and Spread of Cartonera Publishers

For those who are interested in the trajectory of independent literature publishing in Latin America, the founding of Eloísa Cartonera is already a well-known story: Eloísa emerged in Buenos Aires in August 2003 and was led by the artists Javier Barilaro and Fernanda Laguna along with the writer Washington Cucurto. Argentina was experiencing an economic and social crisis, a result of the neoliberal policies implemented in the country since the 1990s, marked by the significant increase in unemployment and poverty, which led to an increase in the number of cardboard recyclers on the streets of the city, fixed in the Argentine imagination as a kind of symbol of resistance in the face of the crisis. In the midst of this context, the creation of cardboard books emerged as a response from the cultural field, initially aimed at publishing works by young authors on the margins of the publishing market. Just as various social movements at the beginning of the 21st century reacted to contemporary policies, that response—and that cultural policy, by extension—was articulated through other forms of production and social organization, such as cooperativism and self-management, seeking to reconfigure in cultural contexts what was determined at the time about cultural production and the ways of structuring work.

As a collective—people who come together through a personal, political, and/or aesthetic affinity—Cucurto and Barilaro created some poetry books with hand-painted cardboard covers and photocopied text blocks. The project, then called Ediciones Eloísa, was organized by Fernanda Laguna, later becoming Eloísa Cartonera. Laguna also proposed opening a workshop on Guardia Vieja Street next to a vegetable stand in La Boca, the neighborhood where Eloísa operates to this day. From the first official publication—*Pendejo*, by the poet Gabriela Bejerman—until now, Eloísa Cartonera has obtained international recognition and has a catalog of over 200 titles where prestigious authors and new talents share the same space. The initial collective became the Eloísa Cartonera Ltda. Graphic Editorial and Recycling Work Cooperative [Cooperativa de trabajo gráfico editorial y de reciclado Eloísa Cartonera Ltda.], which is seen by the group as the "awakening," that is, the formal association of workers of various functions, including intellectuals, occupying a common space and seeking to reduce production costs as they increase collective progress.

Eloísa Cartonera's model is to make the book covers with cardboard, purchased directly from street recyclers at a higher price than the market, and painted with gouache. Following the aesthetic direction of Javier Barilaro, their design consists of leaving the original cardboard visible with all its imperfections, only indicating the title of the work and the name of the author, neither necessarily complete (one of the inspirations for producing this type of book, even came from the self-published works of noted Argentine poet Juan Gelman). The text block also shows this austerity through a simple layout in Word format, both for the works of established writers interested in the project and self-publishing as well as those who faced obstacles to publishing their works. The contents are, in general, transferred by the authors through copyleft—permission to copy, taken from software development and a play on words as a political position in contrast to copyright. As a "social, cultural, and community" project, as they are called, Eloísa Cartonera includes programming other activities, such as workshops, installations, and urban interventions. With such a structure, the aim is not only to democratize writers' access to publication, but, especially, the population's access to contemporary literature and reading in general. Eloísa has published noted writers including César Aira, Ricardo Piglia, Fabián Casas, Martín Gambarotta (Argentina);

Oswaldo Reynoso, Martín Adán (Peru); Mario Bellatin (Mexico); Haroldo de Campos, Douglas Diegues, Paulo Leminski (Brazil); Raúl Zurita, Pedro Lemebel (Chile); Juan Calzadilla (Venezuela); Antonio José Ponte (Cuba); Victor Gaviria (Colombia); and Víctor Hugo Vizcarra (Bolivia).

The Eloísa Cartonera project quickly circulated across the continent, appearing not only in the media, but also transplanted by other cartonera publishers to different parts of the world. Already in the year of its launch, for example, in the Buenos Aires newspaper *Página12* the literary critic Daniel Link commented that it was an "event worthy of greater analysis and reflection than a mere passing occurrence."[1] In 2016, Mariana Mendes from Malha Fina Cartonera carried out a survey on the state of this publishing model in the West.[2] The investigation faced difficulties since several projects arose for specific events or collaborations ending shortly after, some have quite sporadic publications, and others have little available information. Problems aside, Mendes located information such as social networks or websites for 183 cardboard publishers that had been established by the time of the investigation. Among these, 100 are still active. The division by continent revealed that 88% of the active cartonera publishers are located in the Americas, 58% in South America, and 24% in North America; as well as 11% in Europe and 1% in Africa. The data reveals a predominance of cartoneras in Spanish-speaking countries: Mexico in the case of North America, with 23 projects, and Spain in the European case, with 10. However, it is worth adding that, in South America, Brazil is the country with the largest number of active publishers (the survey located 19 up to 2016), followed by Chile (16), Peru (9), Argentina (6), and Ecuador (5). In the Brazilian case, most are located in the state of Pernambuco (8), followed by São Paulo (3) and Rio Grande do Sul (3), and there are some states with at least one cartonera active (Paraná, Minas Gerais, Santa Catarina, Rio Grande do Norte, and Rio de Janeiro). Although there are no more recent statistics, it is possible to verify through social networks that from 2016 to 2020 the number of cartoneras active both in Brazil and in many other countries in the Americas and Europe increased substantially.

---

1   Daniel Link, "Cartón Pintado," *Página12*, 28 December 2003. https://www.pagina12.com.ar/diario/suplementos/libros/10-868-2003-12-28.html.

2   Mariana Mendes, "As cartoneras pelo mundo," Malha Fina Cartonera 11 May 2016. https://malhafinacartonera.wordpress.com/2016/05/11/as-cartoneras-pelo-mundo/.

During the years immediately following the creation of Eloísa Cartonera several others emerged: Sarita Cartonera (Peru), Animita Cartonera (Chile), and Mandrágora Cartonera (Bolivia). In Brazil, the first publishing house of this type was Dulcinéia Catadora, founded in 2007 by the artist Lúcia Rosa in collaboration with Javier Barilaro, who had previously collaborated at the 27th São Paulo Art Biennial. At first Dulcinéia worked with graffiti artists in a workshop in the Pinheiros neighborhood and later with Andréia Ribeiro Emboava, Eminéia Santos, and Maria Aparecida Dias da Costa, three women cardboard recyclers and today artists. As a cooperative, it changed its headquarters to the Cooperglicério, the Glicério Recyclable Materials Cooperative, in the center of São Paulo, where the recyclers worked. In addition to this, Dulcinéia is partially associated with the National Movement of Recyclable Material Collectors [Movimento Nacional dos Catadores de Materiais Recicláveis], the National Street Population Movement [Movimento Nacional da População de Rua] and the non-governmental organization Project Apprentice [Projeto Aprendiz]. In addition to the production of books, Dulcinéia is known for its urban interventions involving different events and projects with cardboard and books, as well as happenings.

Among the Brazilian cartonera publishers, two were fundamental to the conception and establishment of Malha Fina Cartonera: Yiyi Jambo and Mariposa Cartonera. Although there is discussion about whether or not there is a "cartonera movement," it is common for there to be solidarity between projects and for the idea to expand into new formations. Both cartoneras played that solidarity role in the creation of Malha Fina. The Yiyi Jambo publishing house, coordinated by poet Douglas Diegues, is known for its publications in "wild portunhol," a mixture of Western and Indigenous languages from the Brazilian border with Paraguay and Bolivia. The cartonera was founded in Asunción, Paraguay in 2007, configuring itself as the first cartonera publisher in that country. It is currently based in Ponta Porã, Mato Grosso do Sul, bordering its founding space. Mariposa Cartonera, in turn, is recognized as an "artistic-publishing collective" and was founded in August 2013 by writer Wellington de Melo, alongside graphic designers Patricia Cruz Lima and Anna Nova, in Recife, Pernambuco. As will be addressed later, the collaboration with both publishing houses turned out to be essential not only for the founding of Malha Fina but, very especially, for its first publications.

One of the paths taken by cartonera presses is in relation to Latin American universities. In a way, the first publisher to bring this possibility to light was Mandrágora Cartonera from Bolivia founded in 2004, according to its blog, by Iván Castro Aruzamen, professor of literature and philosophy at the Catholic University of Cochabamba. In this case, it was not only the first cartonera founded by a university professor, but its catalog also includes the translation of academic texts with a special focus on the perspective of human rights, in addition to literature and education. Further, Mandrágora is openly against neoliberal politics in Bolivia and has also taken a position against various policies of Evo Morales. Mandrágora also disavows the utopian belief in bookmaking as social change, stating "we only seek to democratize access to books and to disseminate literature." The cartonera model has been discussed by various intellectuals as well as by the second publishing house of this type created in the country in 2006, Yerba Mala Cartonera. Ksenija Bilbija argues that:

> The word *thawís*, the name used for the Bolivian cartoneros, is free of Spanish colonial echoes, which clearly indicates that those who belong to these groups are of Indigenous descent. *Thawís* are those who seek to survive by collecting and selling cardboard. They are paid three times more for the cardboard sold to the cartonera publisher and are also compensated for the hours they dedicate to the production and design of the covers. Mandrágora follows the pattern established by the parent cartonera publisher, but without trying to convert the *thawís* into readers of its titles. The design of some more recent books also points toward more artistically sophisticated hands than those that collect cardboard from the trash.[3]

There are several points that must be taken into consideration, such as access to reading and selection of the catalogue, but for now it is interesting to note how Bilbija's perspective takes Eloísa Cartonera and their politics and projects as a model for other cartoneras. Although they emerge in different contexts in response to other historical processes, they are brought into a broader discussion about the existence of common characteristics of the various projects, collectives, and cooperatives that use (or appropriate) the knowledge and making of cartonera books.

---

3   Ksenija Bilbija, "¡Cartoneros de todos los países, uníos!: Un recorrido no tan fantasmal de las editoriales cartoneras latinoamericanas en el tercer milenio," in *Akademia Cartonera: A Primer of Latin American Cartonera Publishers*, ed. Ksenija Bilbija and Paloma Celis Carbajal (Madison, Wisc.: Parallel Press, University of Wisconsin-Madison Libraries, 2009), CD-ROM. https://digital.library.wisc.edu/1711.dl/PUXN3TYH6FTSE8D

The second cartonera project related to universities is different from the one proposed by Mandrágora Cartonera and is closer to the perspective adopted by Malha Fina Cartonera. La Sofía Cartonera, or La Sofía Cartonera Publishing Center, was founded in 2011 by professor and editor Cecilia Pacella at the Faculty of Philosophy and Humanities of the National University of Córdoba [Universidad Nacional de Córdoba, UNC] in Argentina. The press focuses on the training of translators with a view to publishing translations, coordinated by Silvia Cattoni, faculty from the same university. La Sofía is one of the university's outreach projects, the first cartonera in that scope, and launches frequent calls for the participation of students in translation workshops and the manual preparation of books, including writing editorial paratexts. Furthermore, La Sofía, as with most cartoneras, prioritizes the economic accessibility of its books as well as the publication of authors who have not yet been translated into Spanish. Pacella described the emergence of La Sofía in an interview:

> Washington Cucurto, the founder of Eloísa Cartonera, came to visit UNC in 2011. He was participating in a conference and brought books from Eloísa. Something happened that was difficult for us to understand at first: the students crowded at the book stand trying to buy them, but also wanting to meet the authors. So suddenly that space became a literature class, because Cucurto explained who those authors were, where they came from, the particularities of their works. And that happened outside the classrooms, in the hallways of the Faculty. [...] The initiative arose from asking ourselves—as teachers—what was in those books, why they attracted attention in that way, and how we could bring that experience to the UNC, so that our students could gain experience in a project reflecting on how we think about books, to question it, to analyze it, and to be able to create collective spaces for editing and publishing. From there, we generated this outreach initiative, which is supported by a publishing project self-financed with the sale of the books.[4]

The project has approximately 110 titles published and, in addition to the process of editing and publishing, it also plans book launches and other events around Córdoba. Its catalog is quite varied, with

---

4   Cecilia Pacella, "La Sofía cartonera, la editorial escuela que busca desacralizar el libro," interview by Soledad Huespe, *La Tinta*, 12 May 2017, https://latinta.com.ar/2017/05/12/la-sofia-cartonera-la-editorial-escuela-que-busca-desacralizar-el-libro/

the publication of new and canonized authors from different countries and in various genres divided into collections. These collections in turn are edited in collaboration with teachers and students from different departments and universities. In general, it is a project that seeks to expand access to its works and foster the practice of translation by students while acting as a space for the dissemination of literature and social thought edited by specialists.

As we noted, since the founding of Eloísa Cartonera, cartoneras initially spread throughout South America and later to other continents, becoming both a recognized publishing model and a topic of interest for those who study Latin American cultural expressions and practices. From this rhizomatic network, various intellectuals began to question what ultimately unites cartoneras, beyond the use of cardboard covers. Bilbija draws attention to the photocopied and stapled text blocks, limited print runs, community commitment, use of copyleft and volunteer work, and/or the fact that, in general, all cartoneras are also alternatives to the uniformity of the global publishing market.[5] It is necessary to add that currently there are variations in practice in structure: Some are sewn and employ various other types of physical production. Some cartonera publisher catalogs include authors who circulate prolifically through large publishing houses.

Johana Kunin found it difficult to establish an "essence" of cartonera publishing following her field work with cartonera publishers. More than material traits, she notes "desacralizing the Book," both its writing and its preparation, opening possibilities to rethink the meaning and role of books in society.[6] Similarly, Jaime Vargas Luna, editor and founder of Sarita Cartonera in Peru, describes an "anarchist spirit" as the unifying feature:

> ...I do not think that there is—fortunately—a cartonera movement, and that the cartonera phenomenon as something articulated, with common principles and a logic fully (or even moderately) shared throughout various Latin American cities, is more a projection or an external desire than a reality. [...] In the same way that Sarita

---

5   Bilbija, "¡Cartoneros de todos los países, uníos!"

6   Johana Kunin, "Notes on the Expansion of the Latin American Cardboard Publishers: Reporting Live from the Field," in *Akademia Cartonera: A Primer of Latin American Cartonera Publishers*, ed. Ksenija Bilbija and Paloma Celis Carbajal (Madison, Wisc.: Parallel Press, University of Wisconsin-Madison Libraries, 2009), CD-ROM. https://digital.library.wisc.edu/1711.dl/PUXN3TYH6FTS-E8D

Cartonera considered 'importing' the Eloísa model (born in the midst of the Argentine crisis and which involved one of its icons: the cartoneros, and in one of the most well-read cities in Latin America), to a city like Lima, without a specific social crisis (we used to say, when asked about it, that we had decided to start Sarita because Peru is a country in permanent crisis), without a great reading tradition, and where, for example, cardboard recyclers are not called cartoneros but caladores. The cartonera publishers that followed were also developing their own styles and details; some even, as in the case of Mandrágora Cartonera, in open contradiction with the common features of the others.[7]

If it is interesting to think about the commonalities amongst cartonera publishers, perhaps it is necessary to look at the issue from another angle, also focusing on what distinguishes each project. In the end, it is the relationship between the static and the dynamic that makes for the vitality of cartonera publishing. It is less a question of a mode of production as a rule, but rather of its flexibility in the face of the varied political, cultural, and aesthetic situations from which cartonera publishers emerge. In that sense, the question is not how much it continues to replicate more Eloísas, but how cartonera publishing diversifies, enriching the original model together with broadening possibilities for literary publishing and cultural policy as a whole.

Five Years of Malha Fina Cartonera

As a milestone of university cartonera presses, the story of Malha Fina begins with a visit by Professor Idalia Morejón Arnaiz and her then graduate student Tatiana Lima Faria, with the National University of Córdoba (UNC), Argentina. There, in contact with La Sofía Cartonera, both developed two collections: one of Brazilian literature, *Mar de Capitu*, and another of Cuban poetry, *La Isla de Cartón*. In August 2015, Malha Fina Cartonera was founded at the Faculty of Philosophy, Letters, and Human Sciences of the University of São Paulo, a result of the collaboration with La Sofía at UNC.

---

7   Jaime Vargas Luna, "La rumba y el rumbo: Editoriales cartoneras y edición independiente en Latinoamérica," in *Akademia Cartonera: A Primer of Latin American Cartonera Publishers*, ed. Ksenija Bilbija and Paloma Celis Carbajal (Madison, Wisc.: Parallel Press, University of Wisconsin-Madison Libraries, 2009), CD-ROM. https://digital.library.wisc.edu/1711.dl/PUXN3TYH6FTSE8D

Initially Malha Fina Cartonera was supported by the Unified Funding Program (Programa Unificado de Bolsas, PUB). When the project began, the PUB granted four fellowships for students to work with the project. Later the number of fellowships dropped to two and, at present, there are no funds for the project. Most of Malha Fina's student fellows have been volunteers. The allocation of fellowships has been the only financial support from the institution to the project, which also provided a storage room to use as a workspace. Thus, the publishing house is self-financed: that is, the money to purchase materials that are used in the creation of the books and everything else related to the editorial work comes from the sale of the books themselves, not generating profit.

On the other hand, Malha Fina functions as a cultural extension project of the university, giving students experience with various aspects of the publishing world that they otherwise would not get in the literature curriculum. The first part of the process consists of review and selection for the editorial catalog, in accordance with the four lines of interest of the press: contemporary Brazilian literature, poetry and performance, Caribbean literature, and open calls for unpublished manuscripts by current students.[8]

Some books cross through the four editorial collections. For example, *Não escrever* by Paloma Vidal fits into the Brazilian literature and poetry and performance collections. Convocatoria [open call] is a project that the label developed to integrate more with the community in which it is situated. In September 2015 a call was launched for the submission of unpublished texts from undergraduate and graduate students of the Faculty of Philosophy, Letters, and Human Sciences of USP. These texts were evaluated by a jury of writers and editors who chose

---

8   As of March 2021, the Malha Fina catalog comprises the following titles: 2016: *22 poemas*, by Fabiano Calixto; *O pretexto para todos os meus vícios*, by Heitor Ferraz Mello; *Diálogos e Incorporações*, by Juliano Garcia Pessanha; *Os olhos dos pobres*, by Julián Fuks; *Poesia Língua Franca*, anthology of Latin American poetry organized by Idalia Morejón Arnaiz and Tatiana Lima Faria; *A escrita riscada*, by Eduardo Lalo; *2 ensaios*, by Antonio José Ponte; 2017: *O coração em si*, by Elvio Fernandes Gonçalves Junior; *Crisântemo é um nome bom*, by Mauro Augusto de Sousa; *Diáspora(s)*, anthology of poetry from the group of the same name, organized by Idalia Morejón Arnaiz; 2018: *Drástico*, by Reuben da Rocha; *Cubanologia*, by Omar Pérez; *Caribe Oriental*, anthology of Cuban orientalist poetry organized by Idalia Morejón Arnaiz and Pacelli Dias Alves de Sousa; *Ficções*, by Bernardo Carvalho; *Todo o silêncio*, by José Luís Peixoto; *Não escrever*, by Paloma Vidal; 2019: *Violet Island & outros poemas*, by Reina María Rodríguez; *Magic City: Poesia Cubana de Miami*, organized by Néstor Díaz de Villegas; *Afetos e ficções*, by Mayra Martins Guanaes; *Anotações para o livro do ventre*, by Hildon Vital de Melo; 2020: *Muestra de poesía venezolana*, organized by Leonardo Rodríguez; 2021: *A língua da tribo: seis escritores cubanos*, organized by Idalia Morejón Arnaiz.

two for publication. The announcement of the winners in the first call occurred in April 2016, when the members of the jury were also revealed. The selected titles were *Crisântemo é um nome bom* by Mauro Augusto de Sousa and *O coração em si* by Elvio Fernandes Gonçalves Junior, released in May 2017. On the same date as the winners were announced Malha Fina debuted and presented their first four releases: the works of Heitor Ferraz Mello, Juliano Garcia Pessanha, Fabiano Calixto, and Julián Fuks, also launching a line of Brazilian narrative and poetry. These books were produced as co-editions. With the exception of *22 Poems* in collaboration with Yiyi Jambo and La Sofía Cartonera, all the others were produced together with Mariposa Cartonera and La Sofía. One hundred copies of each title were produced manually by the Malha Fina team. The co-editions echo an important characteristic of cartoneras: cooperation between cartonera publishers and the use of copyleft.

After the curatorial process just described, team members and their collaborators worked on translating texts from Spanish to Portuguese. Some titles published by Malha Fina are previously unpublished in Brazil, which creates a valuable opportunity for student fellows to gain experience as translators. Different strategies were used: collective translation, translation in pairs, and individual translation. The translations go through a review process, carried out by collaborators with more experience or greater command of one language or the other, and the text is then sent to the editor.

In relation to book design, many collaborators have contributed to Malha Fina's output. First Patrícia Cruz Lima from Mariposa Cartonera is responsible for the layout of the first four titles, as well as an open layout workshop offered at the University of São Paulo in the second semester of 2015. Later the graphic designer Iara Pierro Camargo took on the design of all the books in the catalog. Finally, the PUBLICA! collective, made up of five students from the editorial design course at the Rio Branco Integrated Faculties, worked on the project. Editorial design student Thayna Mesa also collaborated with the layout of a title. Other titles have been designed by members of the editorial team itself as part of the training project for the student fellows who took preparation courses with some of the aforementioned designers and learned to use the main layout programs on the market like InDesign.

When the text block is ready, the manufacture of the book begins, introducing its material nature. Step by step, all of Malha Fina's books have been made by its members: purchasing cardboard, cutting, painting covers, printing titles, sewing. The aesthetics of the books have been modified throughout these six years of the project's existence. Initially the titles were printed on the covers using acrylic ink applied to improvised stamps made from x-ray plates donated by relatives. Later feather finishing with paint markers was introduced. Collage has also been used. Currently, screen printing simultaneously prints an image and the title on the covers.

In 2019, another production stage was introduced: three Malha Fina books received ISBNs. According to the project coordinator:

> [...] after much reluctance on my part, in 2018 we got money from the Spanish section to publish four titles with ISBNs, which was the fairest way to recognize the contribution of the team and our collaborators and to achieve results. For the first time the students affiliated with the project took on the tasks of reporting, translation, text review and editing, transcription of a foreign language, administrative management, and event production. So, I see the ISBN as another form of credit since it allows this extracurricular learning to be merged with an academic framework which demonstrates the value of the work of the team and our collaborators, all of them undergraduate and graduate students. It is a concrete example of how we negotiate cartonera goals and values within the university. Books with ISBNs will be donated to libraries and cultural centers that confirm their interest in preserving cartonera books.[9]

In 2016 there had already been a proposal from the Department of Modern Letters, in which the project director works, to fund Malha Fina, including ISBN registration. However, this would imply an expansion of the press's catalog to include the interests of the entire department, which would not always coincide with the interests of a cartonera publisher. Added to that, the sale of books would not be allowed either, and at the same time the publisher would continue without financing for its operations: a short circuit. As a result, the books were self-financed without institutional assistance. After four years of production, with an extensive editorial line including bilingual books by authors hitherto unpublished in Brazil and collaborations

---

9   Idalia Morejón Arnaiz, Editoras Independentes panel discussion, TREMA: Primeiro Encontro de Mulheres, Tradução e Mercado Editorial, São Paulo, 3 December 2019.

with various students for translation tasks, Malha Fina requested financial assistance from the Spanish section to produce four titles with ISBNs, as pointed out by Morejón Arnaiz, as a compromise with the department. Three titles received ISBNs: *A escrita riscada* and the anthologies *Caribe Oriental* and *Diaspora(s)*. The fourth application, for the *Poesia Língua Franca* anthology, is still in process. Up to this point, books by Spanish American authors were published exclusively in Portuguese. That changed starting in 2017 with the launch of a bilingual anthology by the group Diaspora(s) and republishing *A escrita riscada* and *Poesía Língua Franca* in bilingual editions with ISBNs. As has already been mentioned, books with ISBNs cannot be marketed since they were printed with resources from a public educational institution. These copies will be donated to public libraries in the city of São Paulo, fulfilling one of the ideals of the project, which is to put this literature into circulation through various means.

After selection, translation, editing, and printing and binding, the next stage is sales. This is the most complicated part of the entire process, considering the adversities faced by Malha Fina specifically and by cartonera publishers in general, a matter that will be discussed later. This is another area in which the monitors gain experience with Malha Fina: within the independent publishing market, they follow the calendar of fairs and events and understand the book as an item for sale. The student fellows contact event organizers, send a portfolio for Malha Fina, organize sale display, and, the most difficult thing, sell the titles. This area of the book market would rarely be experienced by a literature student without the opportunity offered by Malha Fina.[10]

In addition to the process of publishing and selling books, Malha Fina has had an active blog since 2015 that publishes descriptions of published titles, reviews of other publications relevant to the cartonera community, reports on commercial, cultural, and academic events in which Malha Fina participated, and interviews, translations, and literary texts.[11] The blog is divided into sections, and each section is as-

---

10 Over five years, Malha Fina's books were present in several fairs, especially from 2017 to 2019: "Desvairada—Feira de Livros de Poesia de São Paulo," 2016 and 2017; Festa do Livro da Universidade de São Paulo; LER—Salão Carioca do Livro, Rio de Janeiro, with Mariposa Cartonera, 2016; Feira de Livros Cartoneros: Criações e Publicações, 2016; "Macrofonia," São Paulo, 2017, a poetry and multimedia event; Feira SUB, Campinas, 2017 and 2018; Festival Fazetório de Ficções, 2018; Feira Relâmpago, São Paulo, 2018; I Festival Internacional Cartonera, Recife, 2018. This does not include events such as presentations and workshops.

11 The blog can be visited through the link https://malhafinacartonera.wordpress.com/

signed to a monitor and is regularly updated not only by the members of the press but also by collaborators and interested parties. Many students who have participated in the project reported that the blog was their first encounter with some genres, reinforcing the training aspect of the press. Malha Fina also has a YouTube channel[12] featuring videos of book fairs, book launches, artisanal book production, and author presentations and highlights.

The pedagogical aspect of Malha Fina is the last one to discuss and will be explored later in this chapter, as it encompasses the workshops that Malha Fina Cartonera carried out in public and private schools in the field of teacher and student training. The workshops encompass both the preparation of the book and the creation of an editorial catalogue, layout, and writing.

The Rarefied Book in a Rarefied Market

As previously mentioned the sale of books is an important stage of the cartonera process. Ultimately the press is self-financed; that is, the profits from sales are the only funds for acquiring material, paying for graphic services, and producing further titles, which in turn will generate profits for new publications. However, sales are very complicated for two reasons. First, as independent publishers, cartoneras encounter obstacles to the market dominated by large publishers. Malha Fina has been rejected by many book fairs and events, stating that the publisher does not fit into their guidelines. Second, many consumers are turned off by the cardboard covers.

Broadly, we could start by dividing the publishing landscape into two groups: large publishers and independent publishers. The large publishing houses would be those that respond to the large business groups and that command the book industry, turning it into a factory of products for the masses: the so-called best-sellers that, according to Jaime Vargas Luna, correspond to an "industrialization of taste."[13] This type of publisher fosters a conformity of tastes so that the majority of consumers have reduced options where these publishers dominate the market. It is the end of bibliodiversity, a term also used by Vargas Luna to refer to the various options for buying and selling

---

12   https://www.youtube.com/@malhafinacartonera4864

13   Vargas Luna, "La rumba y el rumbo."

books. In the opposite direction, there are independent publishers. The history of the term "independent" derives from "traditional" publishers that published a catalog independent of the income generated, the so-called long-sellers. This independence in relation to the market and as opposed to the extreme dependence on large, so-called commercial publishers is referred to by the adjective "independent."

In this ambivalence between commercial and independent publishers, cartoneras are on the side of independent publishers, building catalogs as publishing projects of the press and not to meet a market demand. Malha Fina, for example, aims to disseminate Latin American and Caribbean literature by authors not yet published in Brazil, in addition to contemporary Brazilian authors within the poetry and performance series. Compared to the print runs of large publishers the number of copies is also small due to the artisanal production, which makes each copy a unique item. Furthermore, cartoneras distance themselves from conventional independent publishers, which Vargas Luna explains as follows:

> Cartonera publishers do not export their books. They circulate their catalogs virtually and reissue their titles. They sell directly on the streets or at fairs or in schools. They develop new work models that, if they are not successful, are transformed again and again. They are part of the system and yet they remain on the margins. [...] Cartonera publishers are not managed with the same sustainability criteria as a conventional publisher since, in some cases, part of the work is unpaid [...]. In addition, they produce minimal print runs via artisanal printing (or photocopying) on demand, and with reduced costs thanks to subsidies.[14]

As Vargas Luna notes, unlike independent publishers cartoneras do not export, but they post their catalogs on virtual platforms and sell directly on the streets and at fairs. The format is cooperative and, in most cases, voluntary. This applies not only to those who make the books but also to the authors, who make their works available for free. With Malha Fina, no published author is paid for their text. Writers receive copies of their books and they participate because they believe in the project and the potential of this publishing model as a whole compared to other marketing possibilities. If compared with a commercial publisher, even with some independent ones, the volume of

---

14   Vargas Luna, "La rumba y el rumbo."

books produced in each print run is very low, 100 copies in the case of Malha Fina. The impact of cartoneras on the publishing market is symbolic, and the reach of their books is limited. Although it is an independent publisher, it is marginalized even within that universe.

In the case of Malha Fina, there are few fairs in which the press is accepted as an exhibitor because oftentimes cardboard-bound books do not fulfill some aesthetic criteria that independent fairs believe are valid, even for alternative publishers. Cartoneras are on the margins, which is reflected in the books made with materials that are financially accessible to the available budget, which does not always mean the best quality material.

In the few fairs in which Malha Fina is able to participate there are two likely profiles of buyers. On the one hand, there is a public loyal to the press, supporters of the project itself. As Vargas Luna observes, "who buys the cardboard books? [...] [T]he usual cultural consumers: university students in the arts and humanities, fans of the authors, those interested in the value of the project."[15] These are the ones that actually put the project in motion. On the one hand, there are those who, upon noticing that the book is made with cardboard and low-cost materials, reject it. The most expensive book in the Malha Fina catalog is the *Caribe oriental* anthology, which costs 25 reais. To understand the attribution of this value it is necessary to understand how this book came to be.

The *Caribe oriental* anthology, at 88 pages, is the longest in the Malha Fina's catalog. It consists of 18 authors with bilingual poems in Portuguese and Spanish, all previously unpublished in Brazil. The translations were contributed on a volunteer basis. The book also has a preface by Pacelli Dias Alves de Sousa providing context for Brazilian readers in the peculiar universe of Cuban orientalist poetry, unknown in Brazil. Each copy has a flyleaf and an additional cover produced with two heavier colored sheets and with orientalist-themed drawings printed on them. Malha Fina had not previously used Japanese sewn bindings, which our collaborators learned specifically for this edition. The covers were designed by the artists Darío Ares and Marga Steinwasser as volunteers out of their interest and support for Malha Fina. Many of the covers were made with scraps of silk that would be discarded and that Ares collected in fabric stores in Buenos Aires with

---

15 Vargas Luna, "La rumaba y el rumbo."

the assistance of Steinwasser. On a visit to Malha Fina, the artists and some volunteers embroidered the scraps to be used on the covers. Of the 100 copies, 50 of the covers feature this embroidery. Screen printing, collage, and embroidery on paper were used on the other 50 covers. The text block was designed by Iara Pierro de Camargo, again in volunteer capacity. This extensive description shows that the value of the book would be higher than what is normally charged. The sales value is almost not enough to pay the production costs. However, many consumers look down on the product due to its base material, cardboard. As Vargas Luna pointed out, those who consume these products belong to a small group of interested parties, which makes the self-management of the label an increasingly greater challenge.

  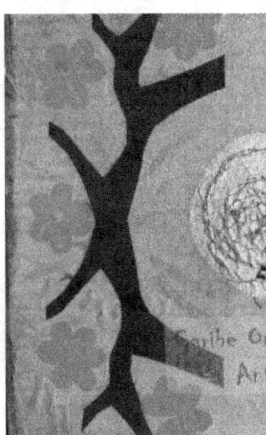

Figure 1   Covers of *Caribe oriental*.

Given the challenges faced by cartoneras in general and by Malha Fina specifically, the press breaks even financially by holding workshops.

Malha Fina Cartonera as Outreach Laboratory, or Other Ways to Desanctify the Book

First, it is important to keep in mind that Malha Fina Cartonera emerged as an outreach project of the Spanish Language and Spanish and Hispanic American Literatures Department of the University of São Paulo, with emphasis on the discipline of Hispanic American Literature and on the research project "Crisis of forms in 20th century Latin American literature and its relationships with other arts," developed by project director Idalia Morejón Arnaiz. The institutional connection was not only due to the affiliation of its members, but also due to the theoretical and critical connection between academic research and editorial work, which was critical for obtaining a workspace within the university and fellowships for undergraduate students. Thus, it was proposed that the student fellows participate in the different stages of the production, editing, and distribution process of the books, as well as other activities of the publishing house not related to the preparation of the books, so that the position can build various experience for them, limited to neither the academic context or the publishing market. Taking this into consideration, a part of the books was made for donation to cultural establishments and another part was sold, without commercial motivation, for the self-maintenance of the project and its activities.

This contextualization highlights the relationship between research, teaching, and outreach, pillars of both the Malha Fina project and the role of Brazilian public universities. The inclusion of outreach as one of these pillars is recent: its presence in the Brazilian Constitution of 1988 (in Article 207, "the inseparability of teaching, research, and extension") is the result of the creation and activism of the Forum of Pro-Rectors for Outreach of Brazilian Public Institutions of Higher Education [Fórum de Pró-Reitores de Extensão das Instituições Públicas da Educação Superior Brasileira], a meeting that sought to provide answers to questions from civil society about the role of the university. The influence is still observed in the creation in 1993 of the Program for the Promotion of University Extension (PROEXTE), established during the administration of President Itamar Franco, then sidelined during the first years of the presidency of Fernando Henrique Cardoso, reformulated in the National Extension Plan of 1998, and resumed after 2003 during the first term of President Luiz Inácio Lula da Silva, in dialogue between the aforementioned Forum and the Ministry of Education. During the administration of Dilma Roussef, especially between 2014 and 2016, there was a considerable increase in the budget allocated to extension projects as part of the National University Extension Policy of 2012.[16] Terena Koglin and João Carlos Koglin show the current scenario as risky for previous campaigns, something that would have already happened:

---

16   Terena Souza da Silva Koglin and João Carlos de Oliveira Koglin, "A importância da extensão nas universidades brasileiras e a transição do reconhecimento ao descaso," *Revista Brasileira de Extensão Universitária* 10, no. 2 (2019), 71-78. https://doi.org/10.24317/2358-0399.2019v10i2.10658

After the impeachment of President Dilma Rousseff, with the implementation of Michel Temer's Bridge to the Future Program [Programa "Uma Ponte para o Futuro"], whose actions were supported by large contractors and sectors of the agricultural industry, by the monopoly of the mass media and by international capital [...], the relationship between higher education and society suffered tremendously. The contingency situation imposed on social policies reached higher education and University Extension, becoming a barrier to carrying out the social function of the university.[17]

In this context, Malha Fina emerged in August 2015 with the following objectives: 1) Create a space for exchange at the university open to the wider community, fostering collective actions with various sectors of society and facilitating the right to culture, reinforcing the function of culture and outreach; 2) Empower the culture and outreach mission of the public university, generating a project that advances the training of members of the university community in outreach activities; 3) Contribute to building the identity of the university, both with respect to its students, faculty, and staff and to the community in general, and promoting within the university a cross-departmental work space that strengthens relationships between the various members of the university community; 4) Promote intra-institutional relations, interfacing the Malha Fina project with other cultural and outreach projects as well as with academic units in fields of knowledge relevant to the project. The common thread through the objectives is relationships, developed not only with society but also with other community institutions and with other sources of knowledge.

Malha Fina Cartonera was established as the first university cartonera project in Brazil, the first independent publishing project as a university course, and, as Adrián Fanjul notes, "the first to emerge in the field of Latin American studies in Brazil, and that is not a small thing."[18] Its concept of outreach is that of the relationship between university and society, especially through research and teaching. Despite possible conflicts with the institution, a university-based independent publishing house is especially interesting as a laboratory for experimentation, reflection, and research on the interstitial spaces of literary writing,

---

17   Koglin and Koglin, "A importância da extensão," 76.

18   Adrián Pablo Fanjul, "Malha Fina Cartonera: Novidade e projeto formador," *Alea: Estudos Neolatinos* 18, no. 2 (2016), 369-374. https://doi.org/10.1590/1517-106X/182-369

translation, and distribution, bridging the publishing market and academia. At this point, we will comment on the activities of Malha Fina Cartonera that are not directly related to the publishing market.

Malha Fina has maintained a blog since the beginning of the project populated by posts of general interest written by the project's collaborators. Other cartoneras also have blogs with different content, but in general they focus on the advertising and sale of books and promotion of the publisher, which is important for various projects, especially due to cartoneras' lack of integration in commercial distribution networks. That is not the case of Malha Fina as a non-profit project associated with a public university. The blog was created to document the history and operation of this type of publisher as well as literary criticism and other academic essays on lesser-known works in Brazil. It also serves as a logbook of the project, with materials on the various events and activities.

This perspective seeks to appropriate academic knowledge of labor and its place in the creative process while seeking to transform it. Fanjul highlights this as follows:

> [B]y involving a large proportion of teachers, researchers and students from the USP Spanish program, [Malha Fina] promises to be a space that reflects and expands publishing as a special setting for various forms of relationships, not just literary discourse, between Brazilian and Latin American Spanish slang and linguistic identities. It is not unusual, for those familiar with cartonera publishers, to find that some of them develop in a university setting or in collaboration with academic groups. Although this was not the origin of cartonera publishing, it is unsurprising that when this connection occurs since scholarly literary criticism, marked by its relationship with research practices, has the habit of fulfilling a simultaneously consecrating and destabilizing role attentive to new forms of production.[19]

Along this path, literary criticism and translation are areas that are in contact between the academic environment and the editorial process, as evident not only in the production of Malha Fina's books but also in the blog. However, they are not always in dialogue: academic textual production employs a language that only that community (sometimes not even that community) can understand, confining itself to a small and

---

19 Fanjul, "Malha Fina Cartonera," 371-372.

specific circle of readers. On the other hand, certain writing done without the support of a theoretical arsenal could give greater complexity to the text. There are problems of language structure, community formation, and access embedded in these silences. The work with Malha Fina and specifically with its blog is in that middle: it asks for the knowledge and use of both domains as a space for the construction of knowledge within the University of São Paulo. This moves its collaborators towards a different area from the academic field of language and literature since they write for a broader audience and allows them to delve more deeply into the area of translation of Latin American poetry, already with a professional sensibility. If, as Bilbija points out, "all cartonera labels try to offer an editorial alternative in the artistically impoverished and uniform global publishing market,"[20] it is possible that the blog creates an area of specific criticism for works published by cartoneras, texts that often clash with the canon to negotiate their place in the market.

Communication to the community is important, including platforms such as the blog and not only traditional paths such as conferences and symposiums. However, the concept of outreach has been understood in a much broader way. Boaventura de Sousa Santos comments:

> Outreach is going to have a very special meaning in the near future. At a time when global capitalism seeks to functionalize the university and, really, to transform it into a large extension unit at its service, university reform must confer a new centrality to outreach activities (with implications for the curriculum and in the careers of faculty) and conceive an alternative to global capitalism.... Extension involves a large service area and a diverse constituency: social groups and their organizations, social movements, local and regional communities, local governments, the public sector, the private sector. Beyond services provided to a well-defined constituency there is also another area of service intended for society at large. As an example: "incubation" of innovation, promotion of scientific and technical culture, cultural and artistic activities....[21]

Santos' proposal opens paths to think about different possibilities of extension projects, establishing various relationships with teaching and

---

20 Bilbija, "¡Cartoneros de todos los países, uníos!"

21 Boaventura de Sousa Santos, *A universidade no século XXI: Para uma reforma democrática e emancipatória da universidade* (São Paulo: Cortez, 2004), 53-54.

Figure 2 *Contos de terror* [Horror stories] made by students at the General Euclydes de Oliveira Figueiredo Municipal School.

research, and acting as laboratories of "pluridiversity," interweaving of different knowledges. The idea of defining Malha Fina Cartonera as a "laboratory" is in the same vein: making cartonera books is a project originally linked to cooperativism and collaborative work. In addition to challenging the sacredness that books still have in various communities, the making of books and the self-sustaining nature of the project connect to action and presence in the field of literature and publishing.

Another outreach activity is training and education. Throughout its years of operation Malha Fina Cartonera has held various workshops at universities, book fairs, libraries, and other organizations and events, but has especially focused on the training of teachers. A workshop was organized within the 4th Pedagogical Conference of the Regional Education Directorate of Butantã, with the theme of "Emancipatory Curriculum in Action: Reengaging the World and Education," in which we sought to establish a dialogue with teachers about the potential of self-publishing projects, especially cartoneras, in the region's public schools. We also held a workshop for the Association of Spanish Teachers of the state of São Paulo on the practicalities and potential of editing and publishing from the context of a press dedicated to Spanish language and literatures.

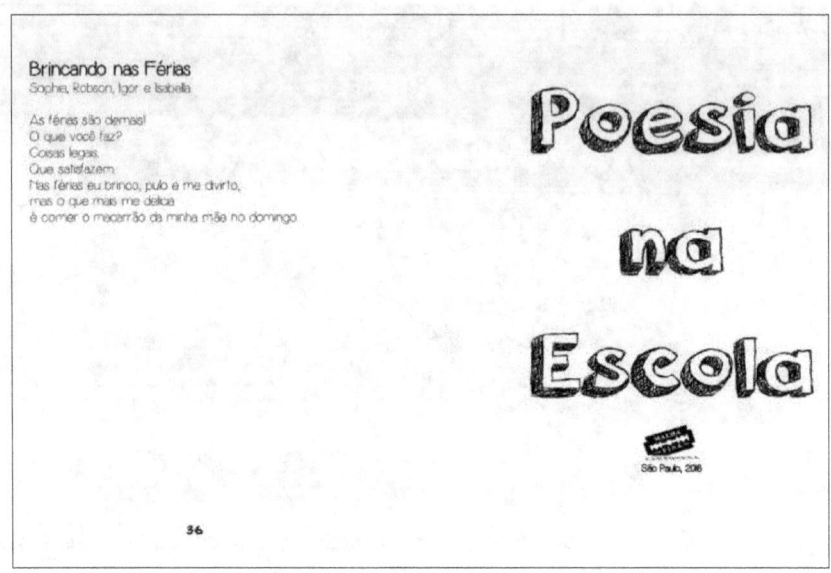

Figure 3   Internal pages of *Poesia na escola*, as made by students at Jocymara de Falchi Jorge Municpal School.

Two other workshops were held in very different public schools within the state. The first workshop took place at the General Euclydes de Oliveira Figueiredo Municipal School, engaging five groups of students 11-15 years old in making cartonera books. The books were written by the students themselves as part of a broader narrative writing project, together with the arts teacher and the Portuguese teachers.

The second workshop took place at the Jocymara de Falchi Jorge Municipal School in Vila Carmela, Guarulhos, for students from the 3rd year of primary school. The students produced, under the guidance of the teachers, *Poesia na escola* [Poetry in school], with childhood as the central theme.

In all cases, the workshops demonstrated the sequential process for writing and publishing literary texts; in the first case, horror stories, and in the second, poetry. It all serves to demystify the book, defetishize even, as students participate in the different phases of writing and the material production of the physical object. The workshops embrace active learning pedagogy (in this case, maker culture and STEAM—Science, Technology, Engineering, Arts, and Mathematics) and promoting approaches to teaching that take into consideration student autonomy. The precarity of the resources necessary to make the books can also promote a reflection on ecology, introducing contact with cardboard recycling collectors and the use of unconventional materials.

Finally, an interesting turn in the discourses on university extension in Brazil may lie in examining not only its social networks, but also the effects of extension work within the university itself, especially within a literature course, with the construction and deconstruction of literary canons, the training of readers and teachers, and beyond the training of professionals for the publishing market. Milagros Saldarriaga of Sarita Cartonera (Peru) was invited by Doris Sommer to offer workshops at Harvard University in 2007 as part of the university's Cultural Agents program, which until now had only organized seminars on specific authors. The workshops had a great impact on Sommer's work, who later offered cartonera workshops with a group of students for local schoolteachers through the Youth Arts for Social Change project. According to Sommer:

> The Paper Picker Press recovers some lessons in creative learning and invents others for a targeted literacy program. The fundamental principle is to encourage students to use literary masterpieces as grist for their own creative mills. Desacralized classics become tool kits that offer up useful vocabulary, clever grammatical turns, and a knack for literary figures. Students exercise their critical faculties both as they poach elements for their own writing, intervene in the classics, and also as they learn to admire the found text as well as the variations of their peers. Facilitators show what to do; they do not tell students what lessons to derive from the creative practices. The students themselves are encouraged to derive meanings from a workshop, for example in painting portraits of a character whose visual image changes with each iteration, or from a performance of human sculptures that represent literary figures of a shared text. To explain activities to students who have already experienced them is to pre-empt their interpretive capacities.[22]

Following Paulo Freire's pedagogy, the workshops sought to build student autonomy through cartonera editing and publishing, placing students as authors and authorities of the books, in addition to exercising their critical and creative skills. In the university environment

---

22 Doris Sommer, "Classroom Cartonera: Recycle Paper, Prose, Poetry," in *Akademia Cartonera: A Primer of Latin American Cartonera Publishers*, ed. Ksenija Bilbija and Paloma Celis Carbajal (Madison, Wisc.: Parallel Press, University of Wisconsin-Madison Libraries, 2009), CD-ROM. https://digital.library.wisc.edu/1711.dl/PUXN3TYH6FTSE8D

and in the cultural field more broadly, Malha Fina Cartonera organized the residencies of the Cuban poets Omar Pérez and Néstor Díaz de Villegas, and the Argentine artists Darío Ares and Marga Steinwasser, along with the production of books, performances, exhibitions, talks, and interviews. Malha Fina also organized events with various authors from its catalog, such as Bernardo Carvalho, Paloma Vidal, Julián Fuks, Anahí Mallol, and Irina Garbatzky. Likewise, Malha Fina collaborators assisted in creating university spaces for the production of cartonera books, strengthening the possibility of multiplying the project. Beyond the university, it promoted open workshops at various national and international events, such as the first Cartonera Festival (Recife), Arts Week at the Federal University of São Paulo (Guarulhos), Rio de Janeiro Book Salon, Cartoneras: Latin American Rereadings (São Paulo), as well as in the series of workshops in public libraries in Trás-os-Montes and Alto Douro in Portugal and in the House of Peruvian Literature in Lima. Malha Fina has organized itself not only through its editorial tasks and catalog, but also as an extension project of a public university with a mission of promoting the pluridiversity of knowledge and establishing relations with society and the university community, for which the cartonera publishing model has been of special interest.

Final Considerations

When Malha Fina Cartonera first began it predicted three major goals and future actions: training literature students for a future in the publishing market, building a catalog, and engaging with public education. In this last aspect Malha Fina put out two calls for proposals at USP and the Universidade Federal do Estado de São Paulo (Federal University of São Paulo State, UNIFESP), through which the press engaged with higher education with the aim of involving the academic community in its agenda. The first project proposed for funding committed to offering two cartonera workshops in public primary schools. However, what was not foreseen was the immense difficulty of engaging with the publishing market as a cartonera press and how much the pedagogical side of the project would become a leading role in its trajectory.

As noted throughout the article, the difficulties of the cartonera model within the independent publishing market exceed those that are specific to Malha Fina Cartonera. The objectives of a cartonera publisher are in high contrast to those of other independent publishers, and its role in this category becomes symbolic as a representation of resistance within the margins. The solution found by Malha Fina may have derived from the large number of teachers and teachers-in-training among its collaborators, including the influence of the university environment in which the project resides. Workshops have become an unquestionable source of income for the project. The workshops given in public schools or through the municipality of São Paulo were free. However, entities such as the non-profit Social Service of Commerce of São Paulo (SESC) demonstrated the possibility of expanding the project beyond the walls of the publishing market.

This expansion effort demonstrates the vitality and dissemination of this type of project and publishing format. In the academic field, Malha Fina Cartonera has been the subject of one Master's thesis and is included prominently in a second.[23] The project's coordinators were interviewed by various blogs and invited to academic and non-academic events related to the topic of independent publishing houses. In addition, Malha Fina's books can be found not only in Brazil, but also in the cartonera collections at New York Public Library and the libraries at the University of Wisconsin and Cambridge University.

Finally, with regard to education: the workshop given at the General Euclydes de Oliveira Figueiredo Municipal School, in partnership with the Portuguese and arts teachers, laid the foundation for a cartonera press within a school environment. Arts teacher Silvia Martins created a cartonera by adapting everyday products to use in book-making for interdisciplinary activities with other teachers at the school. The breadth of this model in basic education has been enormous and, as the student's relationship with the book changes, so does their relationship with teaching.

---

23   Shíntia Gottardi de Almeida, "Malha Fina Cartonera: A resistência em livros de papelão" (Master's thesis, Universidade Federal do Espírito Santo, 2019); Laura Lucía Careaga Quiroga, "Uma leitura sobre a construção do personagem mendigo em três contos brasileiros contemporâneos" (Master's thesis, Universidade Federal do Ceará, 2018).

Bibliography

Lagnado, Lisette, curator. *Como viver junto*. Catalog, 27th Bienal de São Paulo. São Paulo: Cosac & Naify, 2008.

Bilbija, Ksenija, and Paloma Celis Carbajal, eds. *Akademia Cartonera: A Primer of Latin American Cartonera Publishers*. Madison, Wisc.: Parallel Press, University of Wisconsin-Madison Libraries, 2009. https://digital.library.wisc.edu/1711.dl/PUXN3TYH6FTSE8D

Eloísa Cartonera. "Historia." Accessed 30 November 2021. http://www.eloisacartonera.com.ar/historia.html

Fanjul, Adrián Pablo. "Malha Fina Cartonera: Novidade e projeto formador". *Alea: Estudos Neolatinos* 18, no. 2 (2016). DOI: https://doi.org/10.1590/1517-106X/182-369

Friera, Silvina. "Hay un espíritu más o menos anarco que nos abarca a todos." *Página12*. 3 June 2008. https://www.pagina12.com.ar/diario/suplementos/espectaculos/2-10245-2008-06-03.html

Koglin, Terena Souza de Silva, and João Carlos de Oliveira Koglin. "A importância da extensão nas universidades brasileiras e a transição do reconhecimento ao descaso." *Revista Brasileira de Extensão Universitária* 10, no. 2 (2019): 71-78. https://doi.org/10.24317/2358-0399.2019v10i2.10658

Link, Daniel. "Cartón Pintado". *Página12*. 28 December 2003. https://www.pagina12.com.ar/diario/suplementos/libros/10-868-2003-12-28.html

Mendes, Mariana. "As cartoneras pelo mundo." *Malha Fina Cartonera*. 11 May 2016. https://malhafinacartonera.wordpress.com/2016/05/11/as-cartoneras-pelo-mundo/.

Palomino, Héctor. "Las experiencias actuales de autogestión en argentina. Entre la informalidad y la economía social." *Nueva Sociedad*, no. 184 (2003).

Rodrigues, Larissa. "Experiência no selo editorial Malha Fina Cartonera." *La Junta* 2, no. 1 (2018).

Santos, Boaventura de Sousa. *A universidade no século XXI: Para uma reforma democrática e emancipatória da universidade*. São Paulo: Cortez, 2004.

Vasconcellos, Ellen Maria. "Translideração Selvagem: Entrevista com Douglas Diegues." *Malha Fina Cartonera*. 9 Marzo 2016. https://malhafinacartonera.wordpress.com/2016/03/09/transdeliracao-selvagem/

The Artist Book in Latin America
Publishing Practice Within and Without the Archive

Peter Tanner, Ph.D.

This chapter's aim is the expansion of considerations surrounding the artist book, moving beyond its mere objecthood to critically engage with the interstices that these works present, connect, and embody. Artist books incorporate unique physical materials and textual properties from marginal, canonical and non-canonical authors and visual artists, ingeniously translating old ideas and presenting new ones. As works of book art they question the canonical and non-canonical in the history of the book. Equally, as liminal hybridized works they address connections and nuances that exist between history and archives, including what can and cannot be incorporated within the archives of history in terms of objects and repertoire, or embodied knowledge. Additionally, these works present the voice of authors, visual artists, and book artists by means of reinterpretation of the work of other literary or visual/book artists, creating an artistic as well as phenomenological archive of the thoughts of those that collaborate upon a work together.

Ultimately, one of the greatest shortcomings in the study of artist books in Latin America is a lack of development of critical interpretive practices. The development of these practices needs to be simultaneously micro and macro in scope, including histories of print culture from regions, nations, and zones of mutual cultural influence. Sometimes even when there is history present from a particular nation it has often been removed from its context of origin and influence. An example of this that will be discussed is Mexican book artist and theorist Ulises Carrión's

1975 article *El arte nuevo de hacer libros*. More recently, there is a more critical response that has been gaining traction as a result of the lack of reformation of the art historical discourse due to the published and subsequently ossified definition of the artist book. This response is a natural development of this ever-changing genre, and critical questioning of the definition and meaning of artist books is emerging globally. One such critical analysis has come to light in Brazil, which challenges the universalist history that has descended from the hegemonic North in order to situate the artist book in Latin America on the alleged periphery, in Favio Morais' 2018 manifesto-like publication titled *Sabão*.

Publishing in the Americas

It was less than 20 years after the invasion of Tenochtitlán by Hernan Cortés, that the first books were printed in Mexico, even though which book was actually the first printed in the Americas is in dispute. While these European milestones are surely important in the history of printing in the western hemisphere, they often overshadow the tradition of book making that European printing supplanted. There were numerous forms of book-making among the Indigenous peoples of the Americas, including the traditions of the Maya, the Aztec, and the Central Andean record and communication device known as the quipu, which was used by the Inka and other antecedent cultures. The creation of texts that combine and recombine the traditions of both Indigenous and European book-making, with the aid of Indigenous elites and scribes in the service of the Catholic Church's programs of proselytization and assimilation, is the continuing subject of rigorous and in-depth research in art history, anthropology, history, and other disciplines, and therefore will not be addressed in the limited space here. However, it is important to recognize that the history of the book is not one that has a uniquely European genealogy, but instead is a hybrid and multivalent development that is not unique to Europe and the Middle East.

The cosmological need to supplement memory by means of records of some variety, be they scrolls, codices, quipus, visual art, statuary, or calligraphy, represents the need to not only record the official memory, but also the particular experience and perspectives of, at least initially, the most original thinkers from any particular period or place upon the globe.

Such histories are unique and partitioned by history in such a way they can surprise readers and researchers in ways that are simultaneously revelatory and obfuscatory. Jorge Luis Borges elicits this idea of the reader's pursuit of knowledge as being one of both faith and fear, in his poem "Líneas que pude haber escrito y perdido hacia 1922":

> desde el fondo desierto del espacio
> como desde el fondo del tiempo,
> negros jardines de la lluvia, una esfinge en un libro
> que yo tenía miedo de abrir[1]

> from deserted depths of space
> as from the depths of time,
> black gardens of rain, a sphinx in a book
> that I was afraid to open[2]

These volumes separated by history present for some fearful truths that are best left forgotten, but simultaneously permit the fearless reader the ability to plumb the depths of time and space to snatch from the sphinx of books and records knowledge that has been hitherto uncontemplated. While this hyperbolic description of the importance of the book and other written records may seem excessively romantic to some, it is impossible to overestimate the importance of books, as well as other means of passing down and expanding the supplemental information. They represent the sources that have survived for research that can be used in the present to delve into the past and redirect the future.

Among the various types of books that have been published in various permutations, the artist book is one of the most overlooked, though it is uniquely important. One problem that scholars of the artist book constantly confront is the question of definitions. Over at least the last 50 years the artist book has presented a synchronous and concomitant contraction and expansion of its field of inquiry. This paradox is just as interesting as the claim that the book as a medium could be dying in an electronic world despite ongoing purchasing of books from online and brick-and-mortar stores. Despite these claims of the book's demise, the creation of artist books is proliferating with numerous manifestations around the world. The definition of an artist

---

1   Jorge Luis Borges, et al., "Líneas que pude haber escrito y perdido hacia 1922," *Obras Completas*. Tomo I (Buenos Aires: Emecé Editores, 2005), p. 57.

2   Translated by chapter author.

book is one that has been reduced by the voices of many scholars over the past five decades, anchoring it to a specific art historical moment. The particular moment began in the 1950s and continued until the 1970s and 80s, and ostensibly continues today though in a different form, as conceptual and performance art. The critical consideration that was key to the definition of the artist book, as the book format presents a form that purveys a particular "coherent sequence of pages, [that] determines conditions of reading that are intrinsic to the work"[3] that are exist as spatial, temporal experiences that condition their reception by their unique visual or sculptural form that is used to communicate their message. Further, they are "a direct expression of aesthetic ideas in a book form...[representing] investigations of the book as a form through an examination of its material, thematic, and formal properties."[4] They also aim to be "innovative in form or concerned with exploration of books as an artistic concept."[5] These works eschew the textual in favor of a visual art language or a hybrid of the visual with text sublimated. These were not just sculptural books or paintings pasted in books but works that questioned the concept of the book and also had a reason to be presented specifically as books.

The concept was initially the key to this art, not the quality of the execution. That is not to say that these works were carelessly executed. These works were designed in some cases to be ephemeral, while others were created with archival considerations. Nevertheless, a rift began to form because of this separation of concept and craft. Concept as core concern meant that the form and construction thereof were the means of production and merely served to manufacture the armature for the key attribute of these works, the concept. In doing so the craft and skill of assembly were seen as lesser than the conceptual concern. The skilled print artisan was assigned the inferior status of technical assistant. It is this false dichotomy, in which concept is more important than technical assembly, that has been consistently questioned and confronted in the work of so many book artists over the last 50 years. While the examination of this separation is an essential one to investigate, another more important omission must be

---

3   Ulises Carrión, quoted by Stefan Klima in Stefan Klima's *Artists Books: A Critical Survey of the Literature* (New York: Granary Books, 1998), p. 37.

4   Johanna Drucker. *The Century of Artists' Books*, 2nd ed. (New York: Granary Books, 2004), p. 93.

5   Ibid., p. 6

addressed here, the formation of the canons of the history of artist books. When examined it is easily detectable that the primary historic works considered essential precursors and contributors to the formation of this field of artistic, textual, and critical inquiry are all specifically European in origin. The history of the artist book beyond the confines of Europe, the United States, and nascent work in Mexican settings, is sorely lacking.

The lack of attention, on a global level, reflects a deficit in scholarship throughout the world. While the history of printing has been studied in Europe and Asia in great detail, particularly in China, the history of book artistry is wanting. For example, what is the history of book artistry in China? Should the history of calligraphy in China and other Eastern countries be considered as part of the history of book arts for the West as well as contributing to a global perspective? It is well documented that the unique representation of space in 19th century Japanese prints affected both French Realist and Impressionist painters' evolving understanding of representational space on the canvas. Did the calligraphic and printing tradition that was present in China produce some effect in European book artistry? Did calligraphy and printing from the Far East exert a direct influence in Mexico or Peru due to the unmediated contact of the Manila Galleons that crossed directly from Asia to Latin America? These possibilities are incredible to contemplate and deserve attention.

Beyond this history, there are other histories that need redress, particularly the history of artist books in Latin America, where they are known as *libros de artista* or *libros-arte*. These works have received relatively little attention from literary and art historical scholars in the United States, and scant attention even in Latin America. Even such important work as Martha Hellion's *Libros De Artista* (2003) that addresses the creation of artist books in Latin America reflects the same Euro/U.S.-centric history of the development of the artist book in Latin America.

Despite the long tradition of book-making among the Maya and Aztec peoples, along with the quasi-book like form of the *quipu* used by many cultures in South America, there are no recognized precursors to the *libro de artista*. Notwithstanding this clear case of artless neglect, there were hundreds of books that were produced in various styles in the geographic regions of Latin America during the viceregal years and the ensuing age of independence and nation formation. For example, Don Felipe Guaman de Poma's handwritten and illustrated *New Chronicle and Good Government* (c. 1615) meets the conceptualist narrative for the creation of a contemporary artist book reflecting the importance of authorship, concept, intention, and artistry as well as uniqueness in production.

There are many other potential early examples available in Latin America that can be considered works of book artistry. Some of the earliest are the few extant Mayan and Aztec codices. There are many other manuscripts that were made for use in Mexico. The arrival of the first printing press in the Americas was in Mexico City in 1539. Later, the fifth printer to have worked in Mexico, the Italian Antonio Ricardo, relocated to Peru and opened his printing establishment in Lima in 1584. These first printing presses each produced educational and religious works such as:

> vocabularies, grammars, and doctrinal works. Further, the laity as well required the services of a press. Mexico City and Lima, with their viceregal courts and universities, were cultural and intellectual centers, and works of literature, history, music, and science were produced to meet the needs of an educated elite.[6]

Still later, in the Southern Cone, the Jesuits in the Intendancy of Paraguay, after many attempts to purchase a press and ship it to Paraguay, finally constructed their own press in 1700, with its first book published that same year.[7] Many works that are both informative and beautiful were created during the colonial period, both within and without the confines of Latin America, but that included Latin American subject matter, especially the documentary folios produced under the auspices of Alexander von Humboldt, among others. Admittedly not all of these, or the many other works produced, were *libros de arte*. However, that certainly does not mean that there were no specifically Latin American precursors to the contemporary *libros de arte* among all these works. Regardless, given the paucity of those antecedent works that are explicitly cited as precursors to both European and United States artist book production, it is not necessarily a surprise either.

---

6 Julie Greer Johnson, *The Book in the Americas: The Role of Books and Printing in the Development of Culture and Society in Colonial Latin America: Catalogue of an Exhibition* (John Carter Brown Library, 1988), p. 3.

7 Ibid., 75.

Nevertheless, it can be argued that there have been many other works that should be considered and given a place among the canons of book art. Among those that should perhaps be included are José Guadalupe Posada's (Mexico, 1852-1913) prints that were included in various newspapers that are equal to any avant-garde artistic journals and manifestos. Joaquín Torres-García's (Uruguay, 1874-1949) books, which he wrote, in places hand-lettered, illustrated, and published in Spain, the United States, France, and Uruguay, in order to spread his theoretical positions as an artist, art teacher, and theoretician. His books are much more impressive as artist books than any artist book or *livre d'artiste* done by Pablo Picasso or André Breton. It can also easily be argued that his works, where he is the artist and author, could establish his preeminence as the equivalent to a William Blake from Latin America.

Multiple vanguard movements in Latin America and Spain published their own magazines, pamphlets, and other materials to propagate their vanguard positions and attract adherents. The Estridentistas in Mexico published bulletins and newsletters in the 1920s. David Alfaro Siqueiros, the Mexican muralist, in 1921, edited the magazine *Vida Americana* with illustrations by painters like Diego Rivera and Joaquín Torres-García, among others. In Argentina the magazines *Prisma* (1921-1922), *Proa* (1922-1926), *Martin Fierro* (1924-1927) published poems, short stories, and reproductions of artworks, along with critical reviews of art exhibitions, concerts, and politics that share a kinship with avant-garde pamphlets from Russia and Germany in the 1920s.

Regardless of such examples, no figure looms large like a William Blake—considered a key predecessor to the artist book—as a primary precursor to *libros de arte* in Latin America. Most histories of the book in Latin America talk about the arrival of printing presses to the Americas, beginning in Mexico (1539), and then discuss what books were published during the viceregal years. The modern book and the artist book are primarily still defined by the European model, when and if it comes up, beginning with the idea of conceptual art in the 1950s and 60s, leaving out the precursor years in the 1940s, with no deeper historical forerunner in Latin America. These periods are further problematized by the fact that the scholarship favors Mexico, more or less giving lip service to South America, due to the preponderance of publishing and scholars who work on Mexico.

While some works by the Spanish artist Francisco de Goya (1746-1828) are considered by some to be potential precursors to the artist book in Latin America, this potential connection has not specifically yet been investigated and thus does not delineate a specific genealogy of the artist book's evolution in either Spain or Latin America. Unfortunately, it is challenging to find other works from Latin America that are included in the canons of the *libro de arte*, even when consulting Spanish and Latin American sources. For example, while it was Bibiana Crespo-Martín, a consummate Spanish book scholar, who pointed out the relationship of Giovanni Piranesi and Goya's work to the overall development of artist books for the Eurocentric model, she does not go further into Spanish book production or successors to Goya and potential relationships to Latin American *libro de arte* production. Instead, after citing these potential precursors, she returns to the standard Eurocentric narrative rehearsed by Clive Phillpot and Johanna Drucker that points to the work of William Blake as a book artist and William Morris as a crafts-person, to establish the roots of the future conceptual development of the modern and contemporary artist book. There is no other discussion of any other ancillary artist's work in print that was developed in either Spain or Latin America, despite the many histories of printing and publishing in both regions.

The most crucial period for the creation of artist books, which is given pride of place, took place in the 1950s and 60s as a derivative development to performance and conceptual art in the United States and Europe. In most histories, the US visual artist Ed Ruscha's work titled *Twentysix Gasoline Stations* (1963) is considered the first contemporary, conceptually-driven artist book. While there is a preponderance of work that is always presented from Europe during this period, there are dozens of recognized artists from Latin American nations who are only finally discussed and listed by Martha Hellion as additions to the history of book art that were active during and after the seminal 1950s period.[8]

Hellion even takes the bold stance that no one else previously had: She points to a singular work that she calls the only direct Latin American ancestor to the contemporary conceptual artist book, a book produced through the collaboration of Pablo Neruda with Chilean painter José Venturelli, titled *Alturas de Macchu Picchu* and published in Santiago de Chile in 1950 (Fig. 1). Hellion states that "this was the first time

---

8   Martha Hellion, et al., *Libros de artista: Artist's Books* (Turner, 2003).

that text and image merged to create an artistic publication."⁹ This work is significant for several reasons. First, this work situates Latin American book arts at the forefront of the flourishing of the artist book, even earlier than those produced in the United States and Europe by the conceptualist definition. Second, Hellion situates this work specifically within the commencement of conceptualist work as the beginning of the artist book and therefore places it within the accepted canon of artist books. Third, this work is not particularly unique. There were many books produced during this period that have been held and examined by this author that are similar to this collaborative work by Neruda and Venturelli, thus making this just one of a potential treasure trove of works that have yet to be recognized. The distinguishing feature of a work like the Neruda/Venturelli from other books with illustrations hinges upon the difference between interpretation (concept) and illustration (work for hire craft). For example, José Clemente Orozco illustrated a 1947 version of John Steinbeck's novella *The Pearl*, but it is not considered an artist book by scholars like Hellion. The difference between the work of Orozco with Steinbeck and that of Venturelli with Neruda is that Venturelli is not illustrating the poem by Neruda. Instead, Venturelli produces an interpretive vision of the poetry by Neruda, not even following the text, but referencing the region from which Neruda is also inspired, the heights of Machu Picchu. While the book contains images, they do not illustrate or seek to depict the vision presented in the poetry, but instead present a singular artistic vision by Venturelli that ruminates upon the influential words by Neruda, though not depicting them explicitly. Therein lies the question of what distinguishes an artist book from fine press book artistry and the question of conceptualism's prioritizing of artwork over craftwork.

One captivating aspect in the development of the *libro de arte* in Latin America has its roots in social-economic and socio-cultural necessity. This development involved the use of mail art. Mail art began with the practical objective to establish relationships and exchange ideas between artists in distant locations, so much so that "geographical distance was considered an essential component."¹⁰ The use of mail to send ideas and portable ephemeral art back and forth was importantly inexpensive. Low cost was a vital consideration in its proliferation

---

9   Martha Hellion, "Artists' Books from Latin America–A Table." *Printed Matter* (25 Jan. 2018), p. 1.

10 Hellion, et al., p. 22.

as a channel for the distribution of ephemeral art and ideas. An added benefit of this form of exchange and correspondence was the creation of international networks between artists and writers throughout Latin America.[11] This was a decisive factor in the development of non-art object print work and contributed significantly to the development of early conceptual works in Latin America. The fact that the isolating effect of distance and lack of funds were turned into assets, instead of limitations, is an extraordinary demonstration of the diversity of ideas and talents available across Latin America similar to that of the later *cartonera* movement. It is also another testament to the fact that the development of ephemeral art, conceptual art, and book artistry was not limited or unique to the United States or Europe. It clearly presents that these developments were all examples of parallel processes of investigation across the hemisphere and that such work requires more investigation.

Taller Leñateros

The work of the contemporary artist book group titled *Taller Leñateros* of Chiapas, Mexico, represents the recuperation and continuation of book-making practices by one group of Mayan people of Mesoamerica. The projects undertaken by the *Taller Leñateros* are diverse and intriguing in terms of printing practice as well as in their use of sustainable printing practices and materials gleaned from the forest, as the name *leñateros* implies. In this way, their work establishes a bridge from the present that connects with ancient traditional Mayan printing culture and history. Further the description given on the website for the *Taller Leñateros* describes their work as "the first books written, illustrated, printed, and bound…by the Mayan people in more than 400 years."[12] Beyond this possibly exaggerated claim, the fact remains that the work of the *Taller Leñateros* presents the voice and the skill of marginalized Mayan Tzotzil writers and craftspeople of Chiapas, Mexico. Their work is a testament to the power of the arts as a form of empowerment and the importance of printing as a medium.

---

11   Ibid., p. 40.

12   "Taller leñateros–papel hecho a mano." Taller Leñateros (accessed January 9, 2020). "El Taller ha publicado los primeros libros escritos, ilustrados, impresos y encuadernados (con papel de su propia manufactura) por el pueblo maya en más de 400 años." www.tallerlenateros.com/ingles/index_ing.php.

One of the more intriguing works produced by the taller is titled *Portable Mayan Altar: Pocket Books of Mayan Spells* (2007) (Fig. 2). This work transgresses the limits of the book format, including three pocket books of poetry, three sculptural figures, candles, and a box container that also functions as the altar through which all of these materials may act in concerted ritual invocation. The taller website describes this work in the following way:

> The case looks like an ancient Mayan thatched house. Inside, a mayan altar with three small Pocket Hex Books bound in handmade fiber paper, marbled endpapers, stunning graphics created by contemporary Mayan artists, ten little rainbow colored candles, two clay candleholders in the form of animals, and an incense burner, everything you need to celebrate the traditional rituals of San Juan Chamula, Chiapas. [sic.][13]

This singular work from among the many produced by the *Taller Leñateros* is a truly collaborative work that incorporates the efforts of at least two dozen skilled book artisans as attested by the book's colophon (Fig. 3).

The three pocket books (Fig. 4) contain the enchantments that can be invoked through the use of this portable altar and art included in this edition of the book, with text in English and Tzotzil. Each is crafted to appear as though they are self-contained incantations drafted as poems. The linkage here attributed to the power of both word and poetry is incredibly potent.

One example that is particularly telling is the pocket book titled "Hex to Kill the Unfaithful Man" that contains a single poem written by Tonik Nibak. The text of this book is read as a hex, or *hechizo*, that gives power to the person that has been aggrieved and acts against the unfaithful partner. In a situation where the unfaithful man would typically be perceived as having the freedom and power, the *hechizo* or spell provided herein allows the wronged partner recourse to the potent

---

13 "Taller leñateros–papel hecho a mano." Taller Leñateros (Accessed January 9, 2020). "El estuche que representa una casa antigua de los mayas. Adentro, el altar maya con tres libritos, los Hechizos de Bolsillo con portadas de papel hecho a mano, guardas de papel mármol, gráficas creadas por artistas mayas, diez velitas de colores, dos candeleros de barro en forma de animalitos y un incensario para poder celebrar rituales típicos de San Juan Chamula, Chiapas." Both Spanish and English versions are taken from texts on the website, prior to disabling of Adobe Flash player at the beginning of 2021 and have not been translated by the author. www.tallerlenateros.com/ingles/index_ing.php.

possibility of magical vengeance in order to correct, rebalance, and turn the tables on the situation. It is a resource that does not rely upon the mitigation of the laws of men.

This work demonstrates what is concurrently present and absent from the archives that collect these types of book arts objects. While the archive can contain and maintain the physical materials needed for the rituals these objects lack the knowledge to activate them, to perform the ritual. What is absent is the embodied knowledge of how to actually perform the rites prescribed by the poem's spell or *hechizo*. The craft of and employment of this spell by a knowledgeable and initiated practitioner is not specifically demonstrated or preserved by these archival artifacts, even though the potential user/reader can presume that the provided supplies must be there for some purpose.

What is lacking is a form of experience. This form of experiential and embodied knowledge is called the repertoire by scholar Diane Taylor. Taylor uses the term repertoire to signify the skill and knowledge that is contained in a performance and disappears when the performance concludes. It is thus the absent sign or the indexical knowledge that was communicated but is no longer available outside the moment of performance. Taylor describes it as the "performance [of] that which disappears, or that which persists, transmitted through a nonarchival system of transfer."[14] The idea of knowledge transfer by non-textual means is something that should not be new to academicians. Frequently we attend lectures where experiential knowledge is transferred beyond what may have been published in a particular book. Often the knowledge that is richest in such lectures is that which is performed by the speaker, that which cannot easily be transmitted textually but that requires the immediacy of unmitigated person to person communication. In this way the listener is initiated to the embodied experience of the lecturer as an expert who experienced the moment, phenomenon, or ritual firsthand. This type of embodied knowledge, that is often only transferred from body to body, is that to which Taylor directs attention when she posits that:

> If, however, we were to reorient the ways social memory and cultural identity in the Americas have traditionally been studied, with the disciplinary emphasis on literary and historical documents,

---

14 Diana Taylor, *The Archive and The Repertoire: Performing Cultural Memory in the Americas* (Duke, 2003), p. xvii.

and look through the lens of performed, embodied behaviors, what would we know that we do not know now? Whose stories, memories, and struggles might become visible? What tensions might performance behaviors show that would not be recognized in texts and documents?[15]

Her position not only demonstrates that knowledge can come physically to life but clearly manifests what is palpably absent in many kinds of objects collected by archives: the actual knowledge of the spiritual or physical activating forces or processes, of movement or rituals of direct participation, are simultaneously locked up within but absent from the preserved objects. Thus, it is the reader/viewers opportunity and privilege to learn from the physicality of these objects both what they can reveal and what the reader/viewer can discover and invent.[16] Consequently, when the reader/viewer invokes the sacred with this portable altar without initiation, they are uniquely practicing and creating their own embodied ritual repertoire or act of "ephemeral, nonreproducible knowledge." These works, along with many other similar book works, present and re-present the idea that individual people participate in the production and reproduction of knowledge that ends up in the archive, regardless of the elimination of the actual ephemeral knowledge production process (what has been, as previously pointed out, as mere craft). Further, book artistry, past and present provides the unique format to reveal this interstitial development.

Knowledge formation in this fashion is not unique to the construction of altar-like or works that invoke various religious rituals or liturgies. Instead, the work of book art requires the participation of the reader/viewer to activate its spatial and temporal elements. There are many works that serve to present the formation of knowledge by book artists of Latin American origin, as well as non-Latin American artists that work with materials drawn from Latin America. Three book works that exemplify this idea of individual knowledge formation created and based upon materials drawn from Latin America are: 1) Debra Weier's 1981 *Las piedras del cielo/Skystones: Poemas de Pablo Neruda*

---

15 Ibid., p. xviii.

16 This aspect of embodied knowledge, or the repertoire of the object, is further expanded within social historical constructs that include patronage through the concept of achronicity as proposed by the art historian Amy J. Buono in her article "Historicity, Achronicity, and the Materiality of Cultures in Colonial Brazil" in the *Getty Research Journal* 7, no. 1 (2015): 19-34.

(Fig. 9); 2) William Dailey's 1990 *Sky Stones: Poems from Las Piedras Del Cielo* (Fig. 10); and 3) Alicia Bailey's 2010 work *Crystalline Flower* (Fig. 11). These three, unique, book works all began with an examination of the 1971 book of poetry *Las piedras del cielo* by poet Pablo Neruda. While there is not enough space here to detail the nuances of each of these artist books, a few essential considerations are worth mentioning. First, each work presents a unique understanding and interpretation of the materials that they appropriate from the work of Pablo Neruda, and thus represent a form of concretized knowledge formation by means of individual interpretation presented in book format that combines text and image. Second, each work is very different in their understanding and presentation of Neruda's poetry, but despite this each work is activated by the eye, hand, and mind of the reader/viewer and permits them to engage with the work moving temporally and spatially from front to back and back to front throughout the process of examining and/or reading the work. Further, as the reader/viewer peruses, considers, and/or deciphers the use of image and text, sooner or later an unbidden question arises regarding the how these works represent one cultural interpretation of Neruda's work, arguably a whitened interpretation, would be potentially different if these works were considered in terms of their significance to another race and culture, as opposed to through appropriation and inclusion in an outside culture. Questions regarding cultures of production, appropriation, and reception are all issues that works like these require that the reader/viewer parse out to some extent.

Locating Latin America in Relation to the Artist Book

The previous short history of publishing and the several books that have been summarily mentioned heretofore represent only a small portion of the efforts to develop both a historic perspective of the artist book and the artist book in Latin America as publishing practice and expand its historic understanding as visual art and literary object and archive.

While there are many significant issues to consider and investigate further, one aspect that absolutely demands attention is the development of a critical and theoretical analysis of the artist book by both art historians and literary critics. The history thus far of this genre has been dominated by the discourses of art history for nearly all of the last 50 years. A key voice in the formation of this discourse has been

Clive Phillpot, one time librarian to the Museum of Modern Art (MoMA) in New York. His first essay on the subject is titled "Book Art Digression" from 1976.[17] As a librarian at MoMA Phillpot was critically placed to see and interact with the many and varied forms of book art. His work set the stage for what has become a fundamentally formative influence upon the definition of the artist book that was brought to its fruition through the work of book artist and book arts scholar Johanna Drucker's influential book *The Century of Artists' Books* (1995). Though the continued efficacy of the model proposed by Phillpot and Drucker is questioned by this author, it is undeniable that their work is foundational to the understanding of this genre of visual art and literature. Yet this history is incomplete without mention of the work of Neruda and Venturelli. Equally so, it ignores the antecedent influence of Mexican book artist and theorist Ulises Carrión and his influential article titled *El arte nuevo de hacer libros* from February 1975 published in the magazine *Plural: Revista cultural de Excelsior*. This publication antedated Phillpot's first writing on the subject by at least a full year and influenced visual and book art production in Mexico from that time forward and likely influenced others that read his work in either Spanish or English.[18] In this influential publication Carrión publishes a series of maxim-like declarations of what the new art of making books consists of, including:

- A book is a sequence of spaces.
- Each of these spaces is perceived at a different moment—a book is also a sequence of moments.
- A book is not a case of words, nor a bag of words, nor a bearer of words.
- A writer, contrary to the popular opinion, does not write books.
- A writer writes texts.
- A book is a space-time sequence.
- But books, seen as autonomous realities, can contain any (written) language, not only literary language, or even any other system of signs.

---

17 Stefan Klima, *Artists Books: A Critical Survey of the Literature* (New York: Granary Books, 1998), p. 22.

18 Even though Carrión intended his text to be read by writers and literary critics, its reception and influence was instead taken up by visual artists in the production of artist books.

- Among languages, literary language (prose and poetry) is not the best suited to the nature of books.

- A book can also exist as an autonomous and self-sufficient form, including perhaps a text that emphasizes that form, a text that is an organic part of that form, here begins the new art of making books.

- In the new art writing a text is only the first link in the chain going from the writer to the reader. In the new art the writer assumes the responsibility of the whole process.

- In the new art the writer makes books.[19]

Many of these and the other standards that Carrión advanced almost 50 years ago in his seminal article were adopted by artists and book artists, and defined the field, including how artists framed their works, and how subsequently scholars such as Phillpot and Drucker developed and framed the overarching understanding of artist books within a perceived universal history of the book arts.

Alternatively, and more recently in response to the lack of reformation of the art historical discourse since the publication and subsequent ossification of the definition of the artist book, which emerged from the writings of Carrión, Phillpot, and Drucker, other expanded and unorthodox propositions have emerged. One of the most important postcolonial issues that has materialized in the Americas challenges the history of art and book art that has descended from the hegemonic North. This supposed universalizing history habitually situates art and book art of Latin America on an alleged periphery. One recent text that questions the very paradigms of a universal history of art and the culture industry is Brazilian Favio Morais' 2018 publication *Sabão*. *Sabão* means soap, yet this literal translation does not encapsulate what this 31-page publication is about.[20] When the reader finally reaches the only use of the word *sabão* in this text, on page 30, it

---

19 English translation taken from Martha Hellion, et al., *Libros de artista: Artist's Books*, pp. 311-312.

20 It was originally published in 2018 on the Par(ent)esis website and later physically published in an edition of 300.

puts the preceding pages into context as a lathering, a foam job.[21] In this document, Morais describes and addresses the history of book artistry in very local terms, centering on Brazil, questioning all the definitions and standards of the history of book art. The Brazilian lens of history presents a situation where freedom of the press was not a right or privilege. The universal history of print situates it at the forefront of democracy and science, including the artist book's importance to conceptual and performance art. This history of the importance of printing in the west and north is challenged by the history presented by Morais of a historic Brazil where printing, and by extension reading, was oppressed until 1808 with the arrival of the Portuguese king and royal court fleeing Napoleon's invasion of Portugal. Then despite the arrival of the first printing presses with the crown,[22] books and reading were still seen as the purview of the elite, and thus the damage was done, and the book's legacy was established. This legacy, he asserts, is one where the book and reading relate an elitist privilege, a legacy that he asserts Brazil has yet to overcome in the present. Morais questions the validity of the codified history of book artistry that has been sent down from the north as if from on high, placing Brazil and the rest of Latin America on the periphery of its development. While *Sabão* does not pretend to be a detailed history of Brazilian print culture, it does provide a basic primer upon the subject, highlighting the use of illegal printing of books and posters by hand that questioned government policies, insighted rebellions, and was used to maintain in manuscript form original poetic works of Gregório de Matos (1636-1696) for over three centuries until they were finally published for the first time in the 20th century. Publishing, for Morais, thus constitutes a history of guerrilla intellectual activity in Brazil. This guerrilla legacy is one that he believes persists in the present. This is demonstrated by the way that despite the massive publication of artist books by independent, or boutique, publishers in Brazil, that this activity and

---

21 It perhaps even labels all the preceding examples of hegemonic cultural practices and the participation of the intellectual elite of the culture industry as participating in a form of intellectual onanism.

22 This is not to say that there were not printing presses in Brazil prior to the arrival of the court in 1808. There were several printers that worked and printed in Brazil, but the permanence of the press in any one place is in doubt because when printers were present their work was usually limited to pamphlets and broadsheets not books. Morais explains in *Sabão* that it was the practice in Brazil to import books through Portugal, and that even when a local writer had a book to publish it had to be sent to Portugal to be reviewed, authorized, printed, and then returned as a finished book back to its place of origin in Brazil.

artistic production goes practically unnoticed by museums and galleries notwithstanding the establishment and continuance of book fairs held independently in Brazil. Three of these book fairs are 1) *Tijuana* or *Proyecto Tijuana*; 2) *Plana*, book fair and festival; and 3) *Miolos* book fair, all taking place in São Paulo. Morais states that in spite of these undertakings the book arts are not understood by curators. Therefore, even though there is this diverse presence of artist books, created and sold in a city that is a major global art capital, the artist book in Brazil does not interact with, in Morais' estimation, the circuits of the local or world art scene. The guerrilla nature of publishing, which questions the hegemony of the history of the book from the north and the gallery system, appears to be thriving in Brazil, despite its lack of official recognition by major museums or galleries.

Conclusion

An artist book is an incredible object and potential archive on many levels. Though attempts have been made to situate them within a hierarchy of artistic and book importance, it is neither above nor below other works of art and literature. Books have been the tools of art, investigation, philosophy, and existence since their inception. They are democratic sources of information, despite less than equal opportunity to access them throughout history. Regardless of their process of fabrication they are invaluable in terms of both their place in the construction of history as well as the knowledge that they contain. Musing upon the historic expansion of book craft, the antecedents of the artist book, and the expansion of their practice in multiple styles correctly situates the artist book, all artist books, on par with all other art objects and literary works that are worthy of aesthetic consideration and further evaluation regardless of their recognition within the circuits of official cultural exchange. If this exposition has done nothing else, it has demonstrated that there is a critical need for more research in the field of Latin American artist books and the narratives of their place in the history of book art.

Figures

Figure 1 Pablo Neruda and José Venturelli, *Alturas de Macchu Picchu* (1948), 39 cm., John M. Olin Library, Washington University in St. Louis, St. Louis, MO (Santiago de Chile: Librería Neira), Cover. Photograph by author.

Figure 2 Taller Leñateros, *Portable Mayan Altar: Pocket Books of Mayan Spells* (2007), 3 pocket book volumes, fold-out-alter of handprinted cardboard, 1 clay incense burner, 2 clay candle holders, and 12 colored candles, Special Collections, J. Willard Marriott Library, University of Utah, Salt Lake City, UT (San Cristóbal de Las Casas, Chiapas, Mexico: Taller Leñateros), Photograph by author.

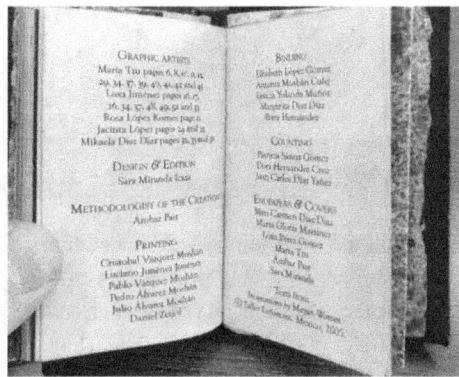

Figure 3 Taller Leñateros, Colophon, "Hex to Kill the Unfaithful Man," *Portable Mayan Altar: Pocket Books of Mayan Spells* (2007), Special Collections, J. Willard Marriott Library, University of Utah, Salt Lake City, UT, Photograph by author.

Figure 4   Taller Leñateros, Three pocket books, *Portable Mayan Altar: Pocket Books of Mayan Spells* (2007), Special Collections, J. Willard Marriott Library, University of Utah, Salt Lake City, UT, Photograph by author.

Figures 5 and 6   Taller Leñateros, "Hex to Kill the Unfaithful Man," Pocket book, Exterior cover (Left) and Title page (Right), *Portable Mayan Altar: Pocket Books of Mayan Spells* (2007), Special Collections, J. Willard Marriott Library, University of Utah, Salt Lake City, UT, Photographs by author.

The Artist Book in Latin America
Peter Tanner, Ph.D.

Figure 7   Taller Leñateros, "Hex to Kill the Unfaithful Man," Pocket book, pp. 38-39, Special Collections, J. Willard Marriott Library, University of Utah, Salt Lake City, UT, Photograph by author.

Figure 8   Taller Leñateros, "Hex to Kill the Unfaithful Man," Pocket book, pp. 40-41, Special Collections, J. Willard Marriott Library, University of Utah, Salt Lake City, UT, Photograph by author.

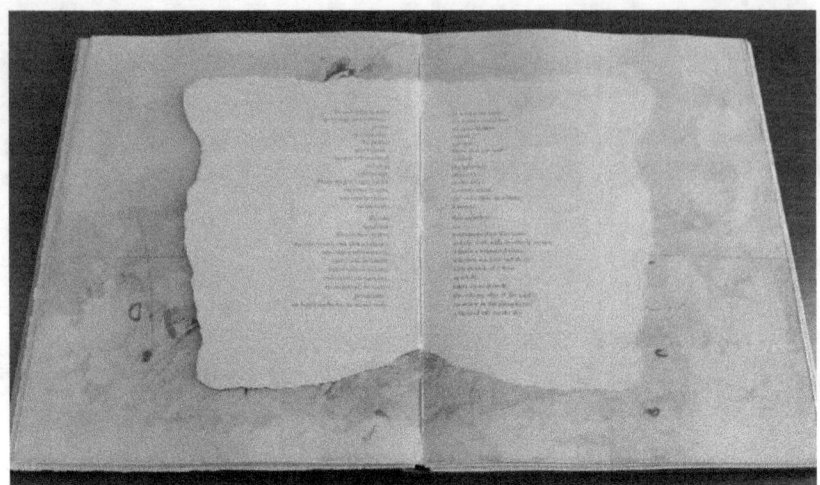

Figure 9 Center verso and recto pages with flap open to reveal/read the poem "I" from Debra Weier, *Las piedras del cielo/Skystones: Poemas de Pablo Neruda* (1981), illustrated book printed and bound by hand, copy 60 of edition of 60, 11 ¾ x 18 ¼ inches open, Special Collections, J. Willard Marriott Library, University of Utah, Salt Lake City, UT (Easthampton, MA: Emanon Press, 1981), unpaginated 16-17. Photograph by author.

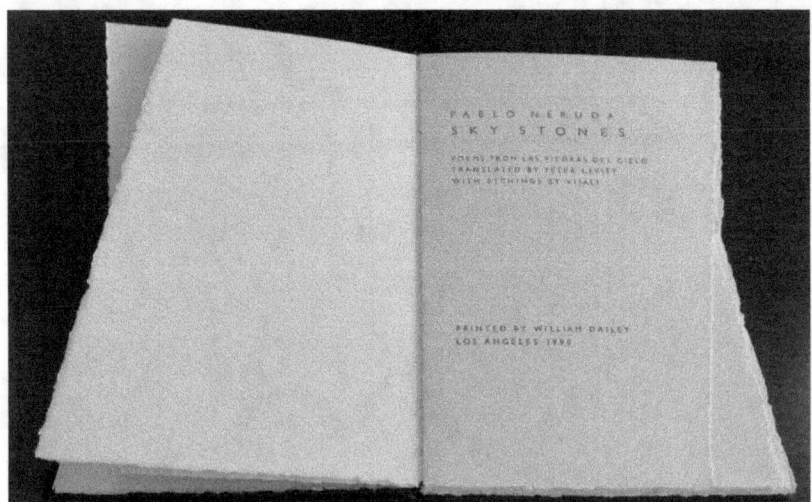

Figure 10 Title page from William Dailey, *Sky Stones: Poems from Las Piedras Del Cielo* (1990), illustrated book, copy 30 of edition of 40, 11 ¼ x 15 5/8 inches open, Special Collections, J. Willard Marriott Library, University of Utah, Salt Lake City, UT (Los Angeles: William Dailey, 1990), unpaginated 2-3. Photograph by author.

The Artist Book in Latin America
Peter Tanner, Ph.D.

Figure 11 Title page, from above, from Alicia Bailey, *Crystalline Flower* (2008), miniature book, copy 7 of edition of 18, 2 5/8 x 2 x 5/8 inches closed, Special Collections, J. Willard Marriott Library, University of Utah, Salt Lake City, UT (Aurora, CO: A. Bailey, 2008), unpaginated 1-2. Photograph by author.

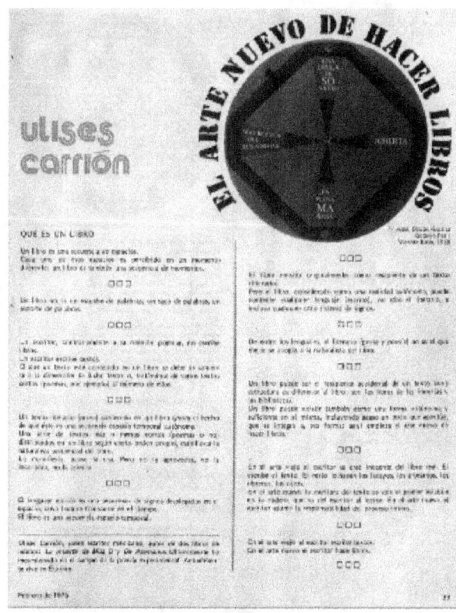

Figure 12 Ulises Carrión, "El arte nuevo de hacer libros" *Plural: Revista cultural de Excelsior* (1975), accessed November 26, 2021. https://monoskop.org/images/f/f6/Carrion_Ulises_1975_El_arte_nuevo_de_hacer_libros.pdf. Also available through interlibrary loan resources with better resolution (Left image).

Figure 13   Fabio Morais, "Sabão" *Par(ent)esis* (2018), Accessed December 1, 2021, http://www.plataformaparentesis.com/site/urgente/sabao.php. Photograph from publisher.

Bibliography

Borges, Jorge Luis, and Sara Luisa del Carril. *Obras completas*, vol. 1. Nueva ed., rev. y corregida. Buenos Aires: Emecé Editores, 2005.

Buono, Amy J. "Historicity, Achronicity, and the Materiality of Cultures in Colonial Brazil." *Getty Research Journal*, 7, no. 1. University of Chicago Press, 2015. pp. 19-34.

Carrión, Ulises. "El arte nuevo de hacer libros." *Plural: Revista cultural de Excelsior*, no. 41, February 1975. pp. 33-38. Accessed November 26, 2021. https://monoskop.org/images/f/f6/Carrion_Ulises_1975_El_arte_nuevo_de_hacer_libros.pdf.

Drucker, Johanna. *The Century of Artists' Books*. 2nd ed. New York: Granary Books, 2004.

Hellion, Martha. "Artists' Books from Latin America–A Table." *Printed Matter*, 25 Jan. 2018, www.printedmatter.org/catalog/tables/26.

Hellion, Martha, Dueñas I. M. Benítez, and Ulises Carrión. *Libros de artista: Artist's Books*. Turner, 2003.

Johnson, Julie Greer. *The Book in the Americas: The Role of Books and Printing in the Development of Culture and Society in Colonial Latin America: Catalogue of an Exhibition*. John Carter Brown Library, 1988.

Kilma, Stefan. *Artists Books: A Critical Survey of the Literature*. New York: Granary Books, 1998.

Morais, Fabio. "Sabão." *Par(ent)esis*, 2018. Accessed August 2, 2021. http://www.plataformaparentesis.com/site/urgente/files/sabao.pdf.

Padilla Aguilar, Alan Gerardo. "First Book Printed in the Americas: Latino Book Review." *Latino Book Review*, February 6, 2019. https://www.latinobookreview.com/first-book-printed-in-the-americas—latino-book-review.html.

"Taller leñateros–papel hecho a mano." *Taller Leñateros*. Accessed January 9, 2020. http://www.tallerlenateros.com/ingles/index_ing.php.

Taller Leñateros. *Portable Mayan Altar: Pocket Books of Mayan Spells*. San Cristóbal de Las Casas, Chiapas, Mexico: Taller Leñateros, 2007.

Taylor, Diana. *The Archive and The Repertoire: Performing Cultural Memory in the Americas*. Durham: Duke University Press, 2003.

Scholastic Cartonera Publishers as a Way of Constructing and Promoting the Concept of Bibliodiversity in the Classroom

María José Montezuma Jaramillo

Translated by Jack Rockwell

Scholastic Cartonera Publishers in Peru

The cartonera movement emerged in Latin America as a response to the transformation of books into consumer objects, and to the difficulty of accessing books due to their high costs. To buy a book was, and continues to be, almost a luxury. To write and publish a book according to conventional means is a significant achievement because of the money it entails and because not all themes, styles, or positions from which authors speak turn out to be attractive or lucrative for the hegemonic publishing market. To cartonear, as Jania Kudaibergen's investigation affirms, "is a more socially inclusive way of making books."

Each individual cartonera publisher has emerged in a specific context and in response to diverse objectives. Some seek to make new or lesser-known Latin American authors more visible or to promote authors that already have a longstanding professional trajectory, and who want to be part of a cartonera catalog because of the low costs of sharing books that it makes possible. Others seek to publish books about specific topics with the intention of democratizing access to reflections on some counter-cultural posture. And plenty more seek to self-publish or to publish books written by their collective, school, or university.

The diversity of objectives for cartonera publishing derives from the diversity of voices and visions that are able to promote themselves through cartonera publishing. Thanks to cartonera books, new authors can raise their voices: people who have an Indigenous language as a mother tongue; members of the LGTBIQ+ community; cohabitants of a neighborhood; patients at psychiatric hospitals; persons deprived of their liberty; children and adolescents in school.

Scholastic cartonera publishers in Peru emerged as a result of the spread of initiatives in school spaces by the first cartonera publishers, such as Sarita Cartonera (in the case of La Ingeniosa Cartonera and Cuskapalavra in Lima), or by the initiative of daring and innovative teachers who, taking Eloísa Cartonera as a reference, joined the cartonera world from the classroom (as occurred with Niñita Cartonera de Tacna in 2009).

Peru has the most scholastic cartonera publishers of any country in Latin America. This can be explained to some degree by shortages: public libraries are in crisis, it's difficult to get books to stock classroom libraries, and it has become a complex task for students to approach writing and reading. But I consider it to be primarily because of the logic of generosity that the first cartonera publishers took upon themselves to pass on. For example, Sarita Cartonera, in its cartonera workshops, not only taught how to bind books, but proposed a model of sustainable cooperative work, recycling, and self-management to shorten the distances between authors, editors, and writers. In addition, Sarita took it upon themselves to provide close accompaniment alongside the teachers that were directing projects, so that they would not drift off course over time. This logic of solidarity is what has permitted the multiplication of scholastic cartonera publishers. The following figure includes a personal tracing of the genealogy that emerged between 2009 and the beginning of the COVID-19 pandemic:

What the cartonera publishers cited above have in common is that they do their cartonera work in a scholastic environment, but they also have diverse characteristics and particular lines of action. Some privilege the concept of recycling and disseminate information about caring for the environment (such as Niñita Cartonera); some publish books written collectively (such as La Ingeniosa Cartonera); some promote writing by way of individual exercises, in which each student publishes their own creation (such as San Roquinos Cartonera, FyA 8 Cartonera, or Talentina Cartonera); others republish texts written by their own teachers (as is the case with Efraín and Enrique Cartoneros) or their community (like Calabaza Cartonera). The fields of action are many, and some of the publishers have a focus on bibliodiversity that directs their objectives.

Focus on Bibliodiversity in Scholastic Cartonera Publishers

Bibliodiversity is the sociocultural diversity of authors, themes, genres, publishers of the system of the book in general. It refers to a necessary diversity of editorial production that is made available to readers. The concept, according to the official blog of El Día B,[1] came about following the creation of the collective "Editores Independientes de Chile" towards the end of the 1990s. La Alianza de los Editores Independientes contributed to the spreading of the concept and its proposals in several languages.

Some of the basic principles of bibliodiversity that I consider to have had a significant impact on the development of children and adolescents are:

- To attempt to highlight the quality of a book as a cultural good and not a mere consumer object. "A purely financial logic pushes the editorial world towards commercialization that is incompatible with the creation and diffusion of cultural goods (and adds to the homogenization of its contents)."[2] This reminds us that access to culture is a right and that books are not only consumer objects (that are sold and bought if you have the money to do so) but that they're also cultural products and therefore everyone should have access to them: by means of public policy, more affordable prices, public libraries sufficiently stocked with books from diverse origins and cultures…

- To attempt to transform traditional circuits of cultural production, in which Northern books travel south, and instead to privilege the position of the South. Latin America is not just a market for hegemonies to reproduce themselves, but we are also producers of fiction and journalism. This means a commitment to disseminating a

---

1 Alianza Internacional de Editores Independientes, "El día B", https://eldiab.org/
2 "El día B", https://eldiab.org/sobre-bibliodiversidad/ (Last accessed October 1, 2021)

variety of ways of seeing the world, through authors of different cultural origins, social realities, and socioeconomic realities, as well as producers of diverse literary genres, ideological positions, lines of investigation, etc.

According to the Declaración Internacional de Editores Independietes, independent publishers play a fundamental role in the protection and dissemination of bibliodiversity, as they are concerned above all with the content of what they publish.

> Their books contribute distinct viewpoints and voices, in parallel with the more standardized editorial stance of larger groups. The editorial production of independent publishers and the channels that they privilege for sharing their books (independent bookstores, for example) are therefore indispensable to preserve and enrich the plurality and spread of ideas.[3]

Cartonera publishers can also be included within the spectrum of independent publishers in the sense that their editorial decisions are often much more innovative and, exercising their freedom of expression, they participate in debates of ideas, aiding the emancipation and development of their readers' critical thinking. I consider cartonera publishers to be even more radical than independent publishers, in that they eliminate the criteria of profitability and financial returns from the logic of their production, privileging the democratization of culture. As it is, the financial component is completely excluded from their editorial formula. As Ksenija Bilbija says, "Cartonera publishers[...] seek to accumulate readers, not financial gains."[4]

La Ingeniosa Cartonera and the Development of Child and Adolescent Readers

La Ingeniosa Cartonera is a scholastic cartonera publisher in Magdalena del Mar, Lima, Peru. Since its creation in 2013, La Ingeniosa has

---

[3] *Declaración Internacional de los Editores Independients 2014* (Ciudad del Cabo: Alianza Internacional de Editores Independientes, 2014), https://www.alliance-editeurs.org/IMG/pdf/declaration_internacional_de_los_editores_independientes_2014.pdf (accessed October 1, 2021).

[4] Ksenija Bilbija, "Carto(n)grafía nómada de las editoriales cartoneras latinoamericanas," in *Akademia Cartonera : A Primer of Latin American Cartonera Publishers*, edited by Ksenija Bilbija and Paloma Celis Carbajal (Madison, Wisc.: Parallel Press, University of Wisconsin-Madison Libraries, 2009). https://digital.library.wisc.edu/1711.dl/PUXN3TYH6FTSE8D

continued to reimagine itself, refining its objectives and recognizing the great impact that a scholastic cartonera publisher can have on children and adolescents in their reading practices, helping them become authors, publishers, and readers of cartonera books.

Bibliodiversity as a concept arrived at La Ingeniosa several years ago thanks to the contributions of other cartonera publishers and friendly independent publishers. El Día B, playing a key role in the development of our bibliodiversity, came to us bound in the striking covers of their books as presented in public spaces and exchanges. However, the concept and the ideals of this movement had been seeping little by little into my practice as a teacher, when I realized the impact that they could have on bibliodiversity in the construction of child and adolescent readers.

If we are all different, why should we have to read the same? Those who develop reading plans in schools select books that are in agreement with the ideological postures that they uphold: books with a focus on religion and morality; books of classical literature that serve as a model for learning certain literary trends; books that treat topics appropriately for the various stages of development of children and adolescents… However, these books are usually very homogenous with respect to where they are speaking from, and even regarding their conception of childhood or adolescence, which can fail to generate connections with the reality and experiences of adolescent and child readers in Latin America.

Many adolescents do not feel drawn towards the stories that they are offered as readings in schools, in libraries, or in bookstores. For example, in commercial or conventional bookstores a certain kind of book is disseminated that might not be of interest to everyone: stories from only one side of the globe; stories about one kind of adolescent as the protagonist, who might be prone to conflict, in love, or otherwise dramatic; European or North American schools as settings… These can be limiting, distant, and hardly generative of identification with the situations in which our readers live. To give adolescents the possibility of encountering other realities, told not by narrators external to their situation, but by their own protagonists, can be an alternative to generate interest, foment identification, and broaden their vision of the world towards a multicultural view.

When the concept of bibliodiversity arrives in classrooms, we ask ourselves, as teachers and as readers: Why did I choose to read this book? Who wrote it? What perspective of the world does it want to transmit to me? Do I agree with this vision? How does this book enrich / complement / broaden my perception of the world?

I would like to briefly recount some of the bibliodiverse practices that can be generated in the classroom. Not all of them include direct contact with cartonera publishers, but they do touch on the fundamentals of bibliodiversity. I have classified them into three groups: practices that encourage viewing oneself as readers and subjects with rights; practices that encourage reflection about the work of independent and cartonera publishers; and, practices related to approaching other kinds of books, stories, realities, and authors.

Within the first practices I include all questions that make adolescents think of their relation to reading. I ask them questions like: Why do they read? What are they looking for in their reading? It can be very useful to begin a process of metacognition about their role as readers. Some read to learn, others for fun, to get to know other points of view, to get new ideas... These questions can also help make them think about their choice of books: What are the books that I choose to read? What are they usually about? Why do I like these kinds of stories? Or questions that make them think about the cultural origin and historical context of the authors of the books that they read: Where is the author of this book from? When did they live? What ideas were dominant in those times? What could the intention of writing this book at that time have been? Does it depict a reality, question it, disseminate the values of its time?

These reflections make adolescents stop and think about their profile as a reader. They become readers who are conscious of their choices, who can have more criteria by which to choose what they read, and identify what they end up liking and what they don't. Questions about the origin of books that they read can generate observations about the best things that books of a certain cultural origin might have to offer, not with the objective of stopping them from consuming them or for them to feel a guilty pleasure, but rather to make them conscious of the fact that there can be other realities that are being left behind, and that it is their right to know them.

With regards to the second kind of activities designed to encourage reflection about the work of independent and cartonera publishers, these can be related to visits to less-commercial bookstores or book fairs of independent publishers, which allows them to get to know works by authors from other parts of Peru, not just the capital. This can also include theoretical classes about the concept of editorial lines and how there are publishers that publish books about certain themes or by certain authors. They can even include interviews with independent or cartonera publishers to learn about their work and motivations.

Finally, with regards to activities that encourage literary conversations about cartonera books on, from, and by diverse topics, contexts, and authors, I have put together a brief account of some cartonera titles that I have used in class that have helped us generate interesting discussions about the diversity of the origins and contexts of their authors.

- *El príncipe Carolina* published by Editorial Diversa Cartonera. An illustrated children's story by Lakita Canessa about a trans childhood.
- *Corazón delineado* by Editorial La Maricartonera. A collection of stories interspersed with reflections about LGTBIQ+ adolescents.
- *Sociedad genital* by Editorial Cartonera Anartistas. Testimony about the transition process of Gabriel Ignacio, a trans man.

These books force us to think about sexual diversity, different gender identities, and the stigmas and prejudices facing populations with non-heteronormative sexual orientations.

- *Escapando de la realidad* by the publisher Expreso Cartonera. A book of poems, stories, testimonies and reflections by people interned at the Nacional Penitenciario Miguel Castro Castro in Lima, Peru.

This book introduces us to the realities of populations that are stigmatized and marginalized by their deprivation of liberty, and encourages us to reflect on the conditions of the penitentiary system in Peru and to understand that persons deprived of their liberty are more than their crimes.

- *Pa Loco tú* by Editorial Karakartón. An anthology of stories and testimonies by users of the Mental Health module of the Fundació Deixalles-Calviá in Mallorca, Spain.

This book makes us empathize with people with mental illnesses. It motivates us to look a little closer into the reality of mental health in Peru, learn about the most common mental illnesses, and to be conscious of the stigmas that these people bear.

- *Chono* by Kené Cartonera. Bilingual poetry collection in Shipibo Konibo and Spanish by the Indigenous poet Inin Rono Ramírez Nunta.

This book introduces us to the cosmovision of the culture of Shipibo Koniba from within, its way of conceiving nature as an ancestor, and the culture shock that someone can have living in a city far from their native culture.

- *Historias de mi barrio: Villa en Salvador* by Caserita Cartonera. An anthology of poems, stories, and testimonies by the residents of the neighborhood Villa el Salvador.

This book allows us to get to know community organizations and the self-management of neighborhoods, as a way of securing access to rights and the traditions of a neighborhood, its customs, and characters.

- *Laberinto de terror* by La Ingeniosa Cartonera. Horror stories written by 10-year-old children at the Colegio José Antonio Encinas.
- *Yo manifiesto* by La Ingeniosa Cartonera. Manifestos written as poems by 15- and 16-year-old adolescents at the Colegio José Antonio Encinas about social topics they are interested in and worried about.

These books help children and adolescents realize that they too can be authors of their own books, and can express their ideas, worries, and interests.

- *100 días* by Olga Cartonera and La Verónica Cartonera. Books originally published on Facebook over a period of 100 days, and compiled without being rewritten.
- *Cuéntanos tu locura en Cuarentena* by the cartonera publisher Arriba del Pegaso. A compilation of stories written by people around the world about their experiences of lockdown during the beginning of the COVID-19 pandemic.

These books encourage us to think that we are not alone in complex processes such as the pain that we feel when a relationship is ended or uncertain or painful moments like those generated by the pandemic and quarantine around the world.

Just like these titles, many cartonera books are bearers of new voices, ideas and thoughts that are different from those dictated by social norms, and which can sometimes be uncomfortable for people with more traditional ideas. However, reading with a focus on bibliodiversity and diversity in general can also allow for the inclusion of many children and adolescents that can feel a sense of identification with the stories. It can even be an open door to the beginning of a process of acceptance and construction of their identity in a calmer, more natural way.

La Ingeniosa Cartonera and the Development of Children and Adolescent Readers and Writers

La Ingeniosa Cartonera is a scholastic cartonera publisher with a focus on bibliodiversity. That is to say, each of the cartonera books it proposes to be written and then published have been thought of from the angle of what new perspective they offer us, what view of the world they want to emphasize, so that it joins the universe of bibliodiverse worlds.

At the beginning, we liked to emphasize how simple it was to create a cartonera book: take a knife, a little bit of cardboard from the trash, glue, photocopies, and you're ready to go. And on the one hand, it is important to make its simplicity clear to children and adolescents, as this places them in an active role as producers of their own books. However, with time we have also learned to give them space to recognize that making a cartonera book is a complex process, as we are choosing to publish something, and we should ask ourselves why it would be a good idea to do it. To help ourselves think about or role as cartonera publishers, we are constantly asking ourselves questions such as: What innovative idea does this book seek to transmit? What under-shared reality do we want to highlight? Why do it in a cartonera format and not through conventional publishing?

As Renzo Farje of Sarita Cartonera, our first guide in the cartonera world, affirms:

> I think that cartonera publishing should create some new contribution that involves its format, but that is not limited to format in its novelty. Cardboard should never be something that makes the project simple; to the contrary, it should make it difficult, in the sense that it should have a justification that fits perfectly with its contents or other specific objectives of the project.[5]

When La Ingeniosa Cartonera was newly created, we were a cartonera publisher because we made books out of cardboard, but we had not yet defined our editorial line: Who would write for us? Which authors would we promote? What were we looking for with our books? When we created our first works, they didn't produce new meanings due to the fact that

---

[5] Renzo Farje, cited by Beatriz Martínez Arranz, ¡Fuerza Cartonera! Un estudio sobre la cultural editorial cartonera y su comunicación Diseño de un plan 2.0 para Aida Cartonera (Valladolid: Universidad de Valladolid, 2013), https://uvadoc.uva.es/bitstream/10324/3777/1/TFM-B.57.pdf (accessed in 2018).

they hadn't been "thought out." It is not enough, then, to put any text between cardboard covers to make a cartonera book: it is necessary to think about how the content and its format complement one another.

When I've completed this process of analysis before creating a cartonera book with my students, I always ask them what it is that our book will do as a cartonera book, and up to this point we have detected multiple possible answers. The novelty, the relevance, or the necessity of a cartonera book can be related to the following:

- This book can't be found anymore, and we believe it to be necessary to spread the word of its author;
- It will be a compilation of the life experiences of a neighborhood, and a medium for preserving its memory;
- The writing style of the stories or poems that we make will be uncommon, and also written by relevant authors (it will be us ourselves!);
- We will make a literary path through our neighborhood, and it will be a contribution to the community, with information that is not easily found;
- We will publish classic Peruvian titles but they will be donated to a school that doesn't have access to these books, and needs them for their school library.

In other words, I believe that a cartonera book really doesn't have limits or prohibitions insofar as it has been thought out well, and it responds to the necessity of a particular context. For this reason, I consider the decision-making process about what to publish and why to do it in a cartonera format to be a great opportunity for conversation and reflection with the children and adolescents that make up the cartonera publisher.

Examples of Cartonera Projects with a Focus on Bibliodiversity

In this last section I would like to compare two cartonera projects that emerged through reflection on the concept of bibliodiversity: the project of La Ingeniosa Truequeferia, done in 2018, and that of Videos de Recomendaciones Bibliodiversas, from 2021 in a context of distance education. My intention is to comment on the stages of each of these projects that had different natures (in-person and virtual), so that they can be a source of inspiration for future bibliodiverse cartonera projects.

La Ingeniosa Truequeferia

This project organized a fair with games that promoted and reinforced fundamental concepts and features of bibliodiversity. The objectives of the project were to explore the concept of bibliodiversity and its importance within the education community, to promote activities that support a culture of exchange and donation of books, avoiding accumulation, and to celebrate the fifth anniversary of La Ingeniosa Cartonera. To achieve these objectives, we planned the following activities:

1. We identified that we needed a place where we could provide information to the public about what bibliodiversity is, why it's important, and what problems or limitations reading only one kind of book can have, as well as when to celebrate Bibliodiversity Day and what activities we usually do to celebrate it. To this end, we did the following activities:

    a. Read information about the concept of bibliodiversity, as proposed by El Día B.

    b. Created a list of ideas that we considered to be essential to understand the concept.

    c. Thought of creative ways to illustrate each of the ideas. For example: to spread the idea that the offerings of conventional publishers were homogenous, we decided to create a tower of books with the same cover of the bestseller *Bajo la misma estrella*, like those they make in bookstores to exhibit books, and another smaller tower with books by independent publishers. The two towers were accompanied by the sentence "If you always read the same, you'll always think the same: an independent book opens your mind."

    d. We prepared some people from the classroom to be able to explain each of the parts of the exposition to the attendants of the fair.

2. We planned bibliodiverse games by adapting classic fair games or inventing our own. We adapted conventional games like Tumbalatas[6] or Pin the Tail on the Donkey, with variations related to the

---

6 Translator's note: The carnival game of knocking down a pyramid of cans with a ball or a beanbag.

world of the book. For example, Pin the Tail on the Donkey became Put the Title on the Bestseller. One of the players was blindfolded, like in the original game, and the synopsis of a well-known book was read to them. The blindfolded player had to be guided by their partner to the title of the book that they thought was the correct one, according to the synopsis, and then put that title on a surface that represented a blank cover. In the case of independent books, the synopsis and the title of the book were read with the intention of generating interest.

There were other games, like Snakes and Ladders, with questions about bibliodiversity and fun obstacles that could occur if you were to venture to publish independent or cartonera books, and Lucha Libro, a competition where two players with masks have to write a story in five minutes with three words they are randomly given by the crowd. At the end, the crowd votes on their favorite story.

Activities at La Ingeniosa Truequeferia event.
Image 1   "Put the Title on the Bestseller".
Image 2   "Lucha Libro".

We planned what the book-exchange would be like. For this activity, we had to investigate how other exchange spaces are put together and make some adaptations for our own. On arrival, each student added an El Día B sticker to their book and then wrote a summary that briefly explained the essence of the book. Then we put them on a large table where the books were organized by type. Players were given a cardboard coin for each book they gave away. To take a book in exchange, they approached the exchange table where they could examine the summaries and the covers and choose the books that they wanted to take. They could take as many books as they had coins; that is to say, as many books as they had brought themselves.

Image 3 Book exchange table.

Finally, as we were also celebrating the anniversary of La Ingeniosa, for each stand of the fair visited (information, games, exchange) a stamp was put on a card that each person had been given when they arrived at the fair. According to the quantity of stamps accumulated, each person could trade their card in for a prize. The prizes were cartonera products: pins with phrases about bibliodiversity and the liberation of books, sewn notebooks, planners with cardboard covers, posters, purses made of recycled materials or Tetra Pak...

Images 4–7 Hand-painted prizes at La Ingeniosa Truequeferia.

In general, this experience allowed students to approach key ideas of bibliodiversity and to think about how to communicate these ideas in clear and impactful ways. They could transmit information by means of games, symbols, and objects, and they were able to demonstrate to many families from our school the importance of reading diverse books to get to know different realities, and encourage the liberation of books, to enrich ourselves through reading.

Bibliodiverse Recommendation Videos

Owing to the context of virtual education during the COVID-19 pandemic, we had to transform our classroom libraries into digital libraries to satisfy the various reading needs of our students. Springing from a conversation with other cartonera colleagues in a Zoom meeting, we had the idea to create a cartonera library where the cartonera publishers that wanted to participate could liberate some of their books by making them free to read via PDF. From there, I decided to create a digital cartonera library on the platform Padlet,[7] and multiple cartonera publishers from Latin America and Europe participated, including La Maricartonera, Olga Cartonera, and La Gata Diabla Cartonera of Chile; Caserita Cartonera, Expreso Cartokanera, Diversa Cartonera, and La Ingeniosa Cartonera of Peru; Dulcineia Catadora of Brasil; Eva Cartonera of Portugal; and Ultramarina Cartonera of Spain and Mexico.

Image 8   Screenshot of "Una biblioteca cartonera digital" [A digital cartonera library].

In turn, La Casa de la Literatura Peruana invited La Ingeniosa Cartonera to participate in a cycle of literary recommendations for bibliodiversity month. In this way, my students in their last year of high school and I completed the project of choosing bibliodiverse books and recommending them by means of videos that were uploaded to the Facebook page of the Biblioteca Mario Vargas Llosa of La Casa de la Literatura Peruana.

The objective of these videos was to support bibliodiverse books so that they should be read by more people in the classroom, but also by

---

7   Link to access the digital cartonera library: https://padlet.com/BibliotecasEncinas/Biblioteca-CartoneraDigital

people visiting the Biblioteca Mario Vargas Llosa's page. The activities we did to achieve this objective were:

1. First, we reviewed some of the concepts that we had studied earlier, about the objectives of bibliodiversity and what characteristics a book should have to be considered bibliodiverse. As we did so, we arrived at the conclusion that the book should transmit a new idea or be written in an unconventional way, be a work by a lesser-known author, be a book published by an independent or cartonera publisher, etc. Everyone chose a book that they had read recently that fulfilled one of these characteristics. Sometimes, this exercise served to help them realize that they had not read any bibliodiverse books for a while, and it offered them the possibility to explore alternative readings in the digital cartonera library.

2. Then, I created a template for a video script that we could all use. The sections that the script had were a greeting, a moment to present the summary of the book, another space to express one's personal appreciation for the book—what one had thought of it and why one thought it important to share it—and then a goodbye at the end. Each student wrote each of the parts of their script, I made some individual comments to help them understand their ideas better, and finally they recorded their videos with whatever tools they had on hand. Some used their phones, others recorded in the application Zoom, others edited their videos with various effects...depending on their knowledge and available possibilities.

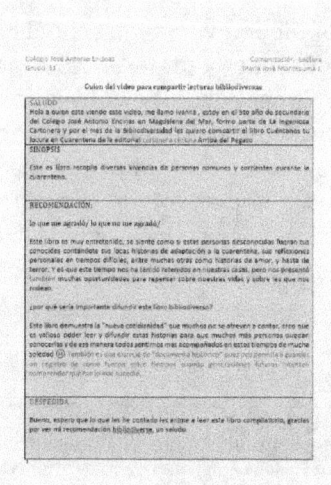

Image 9   Template script for student book recommendation videos.

3. With the material that they produced, I made a website where they could find their friends' videos, and for those of them whose families permitted that their videos be shared outside of the school environment, we shared their videos weekly on the Facebook page of La Casa de la Literatura Peruana.[8]

Image 10   Screenshot of a Facebook post featuring a student's book recommendation video.

This project was a good exercise for them to review the concept and importance of bibliodiversity in the construction of their profiles as readers, and in some cases it also allowed them to try reading new and different books, with the final result of sharing them.

Conclusions

Working and reflecting on the concept of bibliodiversity in schools encourages a process of self-exploration of readerly preferences in adolescents, stimulates awareness of the influence that the conventional publishing market can have over their decisions as readers, and showcases an ample variety of reading possibilities that allow for the introduction of the particular topics, styles, and perceptions of authors. Bibliodiversity as cultural variety applied to books allows adolescents to get to know more than one cosmovision or way of being in the world, enriching their perspectives.

---

8   Some videos from Recomendaciones Bibliodiversas: Episode 1: Escapando de la realidad, by Expreso Cartoknera. https://youtu.be/O5ZbKerHobk Episode 2: El futuro es femenino, by Sara Cano https://youtu.be/t-8LwJ0s2ok Episode 3: Historias de mi Barrio Villa el Salvador, by Caserita Cartonera https://youtu.be/1qDl_Dd2BDo Episode 4: 100 días by Olga Cartonera and La Verónica Cartonera https://youtu.be/G5_iCJGrxpE Episode 5: Cuéntanos tu locura en cuarentena de Arriba, by Pegaso Ediciones https://youtu.be/WZxkhbJiM5I

On the one hand, awareness that the act of editing, publish, and selling a book is not innocent, but rather carries things along with it such as the intention to disseminate certain content, makes adolescents take an active role in their decisions to shape the kind of reader they want to be. For this reason, I contend that talking about bibliodiversity in the classroom can be the beginning of an "awakening" as conscious, critical readers. Recognizing the process of choosing a book reveals the entirety of the path that this cultural product had to take in order to arrive in the hands of its reader, and bibliodiversity forces us to confront the power relations that can also be present in the process of writing, editing, publicizing, and reading a book.

The theme of power relations in the system of writing and publishing of books was for me, as an instructor, very revealing, as I came to recognize the importance of understanding, discussing, and questioning the topic of literary canons with my students: why we read certain books in school, who decides what we study and what we don't, what positions are taken around the universality of a book, and what voices have been excluded from the literary canon of school books, as much as from national, Western, and universal literary canons.

On the other hand, sharing this decision-making process about which books to publish and write with our students offers a worthwhile opportunity for reflection over the importance of the work that independent and cartonera publishing does towards broadening the literary canon of school books, and which books are available to students in general, so that they include a diversity of voices, positions, and cosmovisions. It is not enough to put cardboard covers on any book to make it a cartonera book. For this reason, each cartonera book published by a school cartonera publisher with a focus on bibliodiversity should be conceived in such a way that the ideas of the book fit in well with the cardboard, so to speak, and transmits a message that is complemented or empowered by being published in this material.

Finally, the completion of projects that draw attention to the concept of bibliodiversity in concrete actions of dissemination or that encourage reflection by more people outside of the classroom, put students in another position, and challenges them to find various ways of communicating key ideas about the importance of bibliodiversity to others. It is, in a certain way, a form of concretizing the previous discussions about the relations of power at play in the publishing of a book, the literary canon, and their profiles as readers. To spread the concept of bibliodiversity by means of fairs and exchanges, in workshops where dissident voices are bound into cartonera books, or by making literary recommendations of cartonera books published by other cartonera publishers, are actions that can help nourish and strengthen the readerly identities of our students. These proposals, then, are ways of supplying tools to our students so that they can approach a book from other perspectives than those who support the canon or commercialism supported by big publishers, valuing a diversity of experiences, of realities other than those of central Limeñas, or Eurocentric and United-States-centric hegemonies. Little by little, we are creating bibliodiverse readers who attentively read the story of the books that they choose, but are also conscious of all of the voices that are left behind, and who can act to make them more visible and include them in their possibilities.

Epilogue

Epilogue

Symbols and Narratives in the Public Space
Other Publishing Fields

E Tonatiuh Trejo

Translated by Allison Stickley

> A book has neither object nor subject, it is made of variously formed materials, of very different dates and speeds. When the book is attributed to a subject, this work of the materials and the exteriority of their relationships are being neglected.
>
> Gilles Deleuze, *A Thousand Plateaus*, "Introduction"

On the "new release table" of one of the most extensive bookstores in Oaxaca (the city where I have lived for almost a year) rest, among dozens of other books, the following titles: *La sonrisa de la desilucion* (The smile of disappointment—Tumbona), *Fuck News* (Salto de Página), *Gente ansiosa* (Anxious People—Harper Collins). Carefree and haughty, the three volumes are—there is no doubt about it—very worthy representatives of the long history of literary, academic, and critical publishing that uses the book as a fundamental vehicle for distributing content; as a strategic element of thought inoculation. The three titles temporally coexist with many others that equally collaborate to establish the metrics of a system oriented towards content consumption, authors and brands, and that maintains the pulse of a market that constantly reorganizes the maps and the cultural rankings of the world.

The bookstore is located on Independencia Street. I have come here from the Anillo Periférico area in Oaxaca, where I rent a small apartment with a view of San Felipe Hill. Today the sun emits a rather peculiar cold-heat. The light is harsh. Seen through a "bird's eye," my walk has drawn a kind of staircase on the asphalt canvas, although the outline could also be that of an incomplete word.

I've only been in the city for a short time, so I still devour it with hungry eyes. As I walk, my vision gets muddy—constantly and inevitably—on facades and fences; on clandestine posters, stencils, paints, and graffiti whose apparent disconnection offers a clear and powerful picture of local community resilience. The street is revealed to those whom it is left, as a reading device and as an exhibition apparatus; as playground and fighting ground. I have become aware of the line-boulevard, the paragraph-corner, the neighborhood-page, and while I read the back cover of *Gente ansiosa* [Anxious people]—still in the bookstore—I think that in my hands I hold a tiny pocket wall. A paragraph in "bold" highlights the following sentence: "Getting to this was surprisingly easy. It just took one bad idea. A truly bad idea."

A few blocks away, the library of the Oaxacan writer Andrés Henestrosa has been open to the public since 2003. A "pedestrian poem" (written by Efraín Velasco and marked by Carlos Taboada) adorns the façade, inscribed there to be read while passersby walk around the building (if they start from Porfirio Díaz Street). The black letters on a mustard-colored background share space with a discreet schematic version of the Cassiopeia constellation (which iconographically corresponds to the Marian dedication of Santa Catarina martyr—first patron saint of Oaxaca—eventually creolized in the image of Princess Donají. I think of those other ways of practicing reading: humanity learned to find patterns and to "read the stars"). Inside the library, more than 60,000 books await the arrival of their readers. The doubt hits me, how many of these books secretly wish to switch places with the "pedestrian poem"? How many of the volumes that occupy rooms in this building would like to be exposed to passersby in order to "make sense" more continuously?

It's 11:45 in the morning. My destination is Matamoros Street, number 404. I leave the bookstore. My skin and my eyes take time to adjust to the light, which has not lost its strange thermal contradiction. I walk down Independencia Street and turn right at Porfirio Díaz. On the corner with José María Morelos Street, the aforementioned library appears (which is also the Casa de la Ciudad, whatever that means) flanking me on the right:

"what does the background noise feed on?

that music   the glow

throaty sounds of love   L = O = V = E   its corners   dust

the letters slide   touch of their flesh   dust

we are connection   roses   savage slices   dust in love…"

I am thinking of the different levels of political/social/cultural radiation that spring up in two so opposed bibliographic spaces: the one inside the bookstore and the library, where each publication sold/read deepens the trench that separates intelligence from ignorance, and the one outside from the publishing field where the interaction with the text occurs, in many cases, in an unprogrammed and anonymous way; between an inside that sustains the cultural, art, knowledge, and information industry, and the outside that seeks to make urgent and local discourses explicit; between the inside that receives and demands strategic business planning, and the outside where the publications are at the expense of climatic fluctuations; the inside of the leading roles, the free market, fetishism, the cult of the author, and the fantasy of durability, and the outside of obsolescence, where the dialogic is allowed to be ephemeral, where the editing and publication processes are constantly modified to surprise its readers, unlike the inside where the process is repeated, repeated, and repeated, periodically fine-tuned to obtain the maximum performance of human and material resources in each link of the publishing production chain.

"Inside and outside," I think. I reflect on the reading body as a vehicle that transits narratives and metanarratives which confront it daily from the graphic, the textual, the auditory, and the tactile (at least), and in its natural form will become entangled in fleeting and daily moments of reading. Open moments. Outsiders. The pedestrian poem "dresses" the street, just like some publishing actions of the Brazilian collective Poro (poro.redezero.org), which has been developing projects, gestures, and objects as a means of interacting with cities since 2002. A couple of years ago I had the opportunity to listen to them speak during a virtual conclave of Latin American publishers. In their own words, Poro seeks to "establish direct relationships with the city and its entire communicative complex and symbolic universe, broadening the meaning and understanding of art and construction situations that go beyond the daily use of public space."

Faced with the adaptations of cities for purely commercial purposes—to turn citizens into skilled consumers—Poro counterposes a handful of doubt-seeds: Why not intervene in public spaces to question the urban model? How to help build cities that encourage a curious and creative life, through editorial instinct? Some of Poro's publications have been defined as "radical books," an example of this typology is his work/publication Azulejos de papel [Paper tiles], an exercise that has been active since 2008 and includes a series of images of tiles printed in off-set in color (15 x 15 cm, actual size). These mosaics are glued on the facades of abandoned houses and distributed among the community members so they can carry out their own interventions in spaces that are frequently forgotten by the local governments. The mosaics are printed on newsprint paper so the material suffers the same effects from the weather as the walls on which they have been fixed, and they have already circulated in various enclaves of the Brazilian territory.

Outside, in those non-Instagrammable territories, its falsely dispensable character eroding hopelessly out in the open, it is clear that the publishing canon does not universally make sense, that the notion of reading is a close relative of context, and that although its exercise in public space is usually a commercial, orientational, and restrictive kind, it can also become a fertilizer for denunciation and resistance.

I keep walking. At this hour none of the walls around me cast a shadow. It is the second day of the city's garbage collectors being on strike, the product of the political crossfire that began a few months ago between their union and the mayor's office. The workers denounce the non-existent payment of fuel for the trucks, the moratorium on the payment of their benefits, and the theft of pensions. Sporadically, when the differences worsen, they block the main arteries of Oaxaca with their vehicles. Today is that day.

There are no cars in sight, so I walk in the middle of the asphalt until I reach Crespo. Right on the corner, a garbage truck blocks traffic. The truck rests in the middle of the street, heavy, plastered with political slogans, handwritten union demands and requests for support and understanding from the citizenry. I stop to read the signs that hang from the vehicle. The speech is combative and determined. I try to imagine how tomorrow's front pages will be written. I allow myself to guess. If today's editorial line continues, the heads of the newspapers will invent something like: "Second day of siege."

I glance back at the signs and think about the meaning of "publish" and "self-publish," in the crafty patina that an editorial process can become (sometimes unintentionally). It is not, and it will never be the same, to read about a femicide in the "red news" than to find out about the case reported on the bare chest of a FEMEN activist, for example, the first inside a printed or digital newspaper (an object counts for global reading indices) and the second published on the surface (outside) of a body that represents another body; a fragile support because it is beating and that by its nature is prone to suffer from the evil it denounces, something that is not trivial, since public discourse is systematically and methodically monitored, second by second and centimeter by centimeter. By whom? For what? Under what criteria? The Chilean representative Diego Schalper comes to mind, making a call to the Public Ministry to investigate the young people behind the words projected on the Telefónica building, which began with the 2019 social mobilizations in Santiago. Schalper described them as "miserable" for considering the posts as attacks. Octavio Gana, Andrea Gana, and Marco Martínez (members of Delight Lab, the audiovisual design studio behind the "light manifesto") began receiving threatening messages after his incendiary remarks. "We fear for our physical safety, and we request the support of the cultural community and all those who share democratic values and respect for human rights. [...] The statements of the deputy [Schalper] are violent, which is not what we do, and someone could even interpret them as an incitement to the persecutions and intimidation which we are suffering," the three declared before the media after their website was hacked.[1]

During the week of October 19 to 25 of that year, Delight Lab projected the following words and phrases in full view of the whole world: "Dignidad!!" (Dignity!!), "No Estamos en guerra. Estamos unidos" [We are not at war. We are united.], "¿Dónde está la razón?" [Where is the reasoning?], "Que sus rostros cubran el horizonte" [May their faces cover the horizon—a verse by the local poet Raúl Zurita], "¿Qué entiende Ud. por Democracia?" [What do you understand by Democracy?],

---

1   Delight Lab's full statement is included in "Habla Delight Lab, el equipo tras las intervenciones en la Telefónica: 'Nunca ha sido el espíritu llamar a la violencia'," Chilevisión, 20 May 2020, https://www.chilevision.cl/noticias/historias/entrevista/habla-delight-lab-el-equipo-tras-las-intervenciones-en-la-telefonica

"Chile despertó" [Chile has woken], and "Por un nuevo país" [For a new country], all about an architecture that represented—at the time—the graduation of Santiago as a modern city, ready for tall skyscrapers in the shape of household appliances. From the editorial field, much has been written and talked about the prevalence of discourse, but there is added power in choosing the appropriate vehicle, material and technique to fix, even temporarily, each content. To project writing on the Telefónica building was to publish on a symbol. Writing with light was unheard of poetics. The alignment of decisions after that publication resulted in a socialized reading experience that could be understood from its container as well as from its content, forming a "molecular" association between the two that was sealed in the reading experience. These publications were so uncomfortable for some that one afternoon a truck appeared with powerful reflectors to wash them out (also with light, in a sadly lyrical way). That truck, according to some testimonies published on YouTube, arrived under escort and was protected by a group of police officers. Nobody, of course, took responsibility for that attack.

Barely three days after the social mobilizations began, Sebastián Piñera, President of Chile, declared: "We are at war against a powerful, ruthless enemy, who does not respect anything or anyone, willing to use violence and crime without any limit [...]; willing to burn down our hospitals and our subway stations, with the sole purpose of doing as much damage as possible."[2] That "powerful enemy" was the same society that Piñera addressed on TV, and the answer came through a publication as beautiful as it was precarious: a small fanzine, printed on a single sheet of paper, which was reproduced by thousands, and it circulated from hand to hand during the first weeks of protests. Its content: a single sentence: "We are not at war. We are in love."

During the following months after the first expressions of repudiation of the Piñera government, the streets of Chile forged into a lively and open publication. "We didn't leave a square centimeter without our expression," the illustrator Carla Vaccaro told me very recently—without exaggerating, I think. The record of this great graphic production in turn generated a handful of publications around the world. Two in Mexico particularly call my attention: Resistencia (Resistance) from the T.e.l.a.r. (also based here in Oaxaca and managed by the lovely

---

2   Sebastián Piñera, nationally televised address, 19 October 2019.

Erandi Adame) and another that stands out for its bipolarity, Imprimir es resistir [To print is to resist] from Gato Negro Ediciones (www.gatonegro.ninja), since each page is a copy of a poster at original size. The publication is designed so that the posters can be detached and used again. It is a book that lives (which is) inside and outside.

Slowly, but without stopping to read the union demands of the cleaning workers, I move past the truck that chokes the street. I continue my way over Sabino Crespo. Manuel Sabino Crespo was a New Spanish Catholic priest who, by his own decision, joined the Mexican independence movement when José María Morelos captured Oaxaca in 1812. That is why it makes sense that Morelos Street intersects with Crespo Street: in this country the names of the streets also tell stories, and many of them support the official historical narrative. There is, for example, the Paseo de La Reforma (in Mexico City), one of the most emblematic avenues—perhaps the most—of the country's capital, which for some time has been part (victim, some would say) of the installation of a popular counter-rhetoric that little by little has been changing its original face and meaning. Let me explain. Originally called Paseo de la Emperatriz or Paseo del Emperador (since it was commissioned by Maximilian I of Mexico during the Second Mexican Empire), the throughway today owes its name to the fact that the government of Sebastián Lerdo de Tejada (1872-1876) decided to honor the "Benemérito de las Américas," Benito Juárez (Oaxacan, by the way). In its line from east to west, the avenue supports a nationalist discourse based on various sculptures and monuments that were placed to tell the story of the Mexican epic. The statue of Christopher Columbus stood as the beginning of said gloss, followed by the statue of Cuauhtémoc as a representation of the fervent neo-indigenism of Emperor Maximilian. The "Angel of Independence," donated by the French government 100 years after the separation of Mexico from the Spanish crown, is the next monumental piece and the epicenter of the tour (it is also the most recurring place for popular celebrations, as well as a meeting point for protest rallies and social denunciation). Further on, at the intersection of Reforma and Río Misisipi, Diana the Huntress rises, a naked female representing the Greek goddess Artemis, placed on the avenue in 1942 in tune with the muralist movement, as a representative element of socialist realism. (The statue would live its own episode of censorship a year after its unveiling, when the sculptor Juan F. Olaguíbel was forced to cast a bronze loincloth for it to preserve its public exposure. Among the citizens most outraged by Diana's nudity were the members of a group as colorful as it was powerful: the League of Decency. Diana would not return to being naked again until 1968.) The Estela de Luz, nicknamed by the inhabitants of the city as "Estela of Corruption," an elevated monument to celebrate the bicentennial of Independence and the centennial of the Revolution in 2010, completes the collection of bombastic symbols with its climax in front of the "Door of the Lions," entrance to the forest of Chapultepec. We can "read" the Paseo de la Reforma as if it were an official history book.

In general, when these stone or metal masses are affected during the social mobilizations that flow towards the central square of the city, they are the object of restorations to maintain a salable urban face (around here they say "in bad weather, a good face"). However, due to the growing social discontent and the exponential severity of tragedies and harassment against specific and minority sectors, the Paseo de la Reforma has undergone a dialogical reconfiguration (it could be said brutal, but I prefer to call it natural). A little over a year ago, just before I moved to Oaxaca, in addition to the visible popular intervention/argumentation poured over the surfaces of each one of these monuments—which looked wounded, sad, and, frankly, exhausted—a new generation had already settled of permanent "anti-monuments" that now flank the avenue or rest on its central ridge.

Each "anti-monument" was strategically placed by civil society in front of some emblem of the Mexicanist historical demagogy. The first of them was erected on April 26, 2015, following the disappearance of 43 students from the Ayotzinapa Escuela Normal Rural (2014). In those days, CDMX became a meeting point to demand the young people be presented alive or, failing that, justice be presented to those responsible for their murder. It was the parents of the "normalistas" who installed a "+43" requesting clarification of the case that, to date, remains unresolved. It is located at the junction between Reforma and Avenida de La República in front of the Monument to the Revolution.

On June 5, 2009, in Hermosillo, Sonora, a fire at the ABC daycare center killed 49 children and seriously injured another 109. The day care center was subrogated by the Mexican Institute of Social Safety. On June 5, 2017, eight years after the tragedy, the parents of the victims installed an "anti-monument" outside the headquarters of said institution, located on Paseo de La Reforma, to demand justice for the deaths of the 49 babies.

On January 5, 2018, a new "anti-monument" was installed, this time as a reminder of two young people (David Ramírez and Miguel Rivera) who were kidnapped on a highway in the state of Guerrero (2015) when they were going to vacation in the port of Ixtapa Zihuatanejo. They are still missing. The reminder was prostrated in front of the National Lottery building.

On February 19, 2018, two years after 63 miners were buried in the Pasta de Conchos mine, in the state of Coahuila, friends and relatives installed the "anti-monument +65" in front of the Mexican Stock Exchange, in CDMX, demanding that those responsible for the precarious security and maintenance conditions that led to the underground accident be presented.

On March 8, 2019, International Women's Day, the "Ni una más anti-monument" was installed by activists and feminist groups on Avenida Juárez in CDMX right in front of the emblematic Palace of Fine Arts. This "anti-monument" includes the inscription "In Mexico 9 women are murdered a day," written on the symbol of the female sex.

On August 22, 2020, in front of the United States embassy, the "+72 anti-monument" was placed, in protest of the massacre in San Fernando, Tamaulipas, where 58 migrant men and 14 women were killed by organized crime.

To one side of the Metropolitan Cathedral, on the edge of the Plaza de la Constitución, rests another "anti-monument" that recalls the massacre of students by the Mexican army, on October 2, 1968, in Tlatelolco, Mexico City. Three years later, in 1971, the federal government once again orchestrated a massacre of students. This incident is known as the "Halconazo." The "anti-monument to the Halconazo" was fixed at the corner of Avenida Juárez and Humboldt, on July 10, 2021, in commemoration of the 50th anniversary of government disloyalty.

In relation to the massacre of 1968 and public space as a field of debate, ¡El móndrigo! comes to mind, an apocryphal propaganda book published by the non-existent publishing house Alba Roja (its publication is attributed to the Ministry of the Interior or the Federal Directorate of Security of the Government of Mexico; it is not known for sure) to justify ideologically within society the state terrorism exercised against the students of that time. The text, written in the form of an intimate diary, increased paranoia about a socialist invasion, described the violent temper of the National Strike Council, its coup aspirations, and a virulent anti-Mexican discourse on the part of its adherents. According to an explanatory note included at the beginning of the book, the original file was found inside the backpack of a student leader who died on October 2 in the Chihuahua de Tlatelolco building. As the clarification continues, the text was published without a single modification, so in its margins rest notes and annotations in the handwriting of its "author". Once printed, ¡El móndrigo! was distributed for free in cinemas, markets, or was left strategically abandoned in public areas around the country. The book is, without a doubt, a powerful tool; invariably political.

All the "anti-monuments" are united first by their bitter motivation, although a certain uniformity is also visible regarding their sizes, shapes, and materials. There is a plastic/aesthetic congruence in the popular narrative thread; a kind of "style manual" that permeates all of the "anti-monuments." These new symbols accompany the passerby during his daily galivants and coexist with the vestiges of the former national glory. The Columbus Monument shines above the rest...but it does so by its absence. The "discoverer of America" was officially removed from his site after a popular call to take him down went viral on social media on October 11, 2020. He will not return. In his place will be a statue-tribute to the Indigenous woman. This is how history is rewritten. Publishing is rewriting.

I am thinking of Deleuze, in the introduction to his *A Thousand Plateaus*:

> In a book, as in anything else, there are lines of articulation or segmentation, strata, lines of flight, movements of de-stratification. A book is a multiplicity. There is no difference between what a book talks about and how it is made. You never have to ask what a book means, signified or signifier, in a book there is nothing to understand, you just have to ask yourself what it works with, in connection with what it makes intensities pass through or not, into what multiplicities it introduces and metamorphoses its own.[3]

The book is not only the object, it is everything that passes through it, and it does not behave like a particle, it behaves like a wave. This is how editorial thought jumps off the page onto a terrain where more or less predictable relationships are interwoven, barely discernible for some. It leaves the two dimensions to accommodate itself in the public space, where it dissolves between editing the territory, the process

---

3   Gilles Deleuze and Félix Guattari, *Mille plateaux* (Paris : Éditions de Minuit, 1980).

attached to the cartographic and symbolic characteristics of the terrain, the syntax and the phenomenology of the space, ready to fan the fire of the narratives. The book no longer inhabits its body, it wanders detached, outside its morphology and that ether, its ether, dances or fights hand-to-hand with the reader/spectator.

I continue walking on Sabino Crespo. I can already see my destination. From a "bird's eye view" my route extended its stair shape and now it looks more like one of those fretworks that adorn the buildings in the archaeological zone of Mitla, less than an hour from here. Do I write while walking? I have left these reflections scattered throughout the streets of Oaxaca. Although no one can see them, they have the following form:

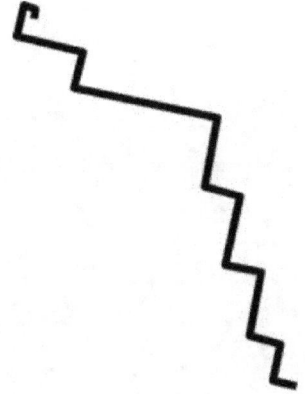

Agradecimientos

The editors wish to thank the contributing authors for their work in putting their thoughts and experiences to words. Not all of them are in jobs that reward publication, which we wish to recognize. The editors thank Paloma Celis Carbajal, Jack Rockwell, and Allison Stickley for their translations. We also thank the Friends of the University of Iowa Libraries for generously funding the translations by Rockwell and Stickley.

The following chapters appeared previously elsewhere. Our thanks to the authors, Mariana Sáez and Francisco Magallanes of Club Hem, and Simón Ergas and Galo Ghigliotto of La Furia del Libro.

"The act of reading is immersed in a net woven by colonialism" originally appeared as "Los actos de lectura están inmersos en una red tejida por el colonialismo" in *Un nosotrxs sin estado* (Valencia; Chiapas: Ediciones OnA, 2018).

"How to prepare yourself for the collapse of the industrial publishing system" previously appeared in *World Literature Today* 95, no. 2 (spring 2021) in English. The original Spanish, "Cómo prepararse para el colapso del sistema industrial de publicación," was published by Oficina Perambulante (La Plata, 2020).

"The imperfect edition" and "Collaborative distribution" originally appeared in Spanish as "La edición imperfecta" and "La distribución asociada: Alianzas contingentes y proyectos consolidados," respectively, in *Estado de feria permanente: La experiencia de las editoriales independientes argentinas, 2001-2020*, edited by Daniel Badenes and Verónica Stedile Luna (La Plata: Club Hem, 2019).

"What is an independent publisher?" originally appeared as "¿Qué es una editorial independiente?" in *El Mostrador* (4 December 2013).

Contributor Bios

Yásnaya Aguilar Gil (Ayutla Mixe) is a member of Colectivo Mixe (COL-MIX), a collective of Mixe youth that undertake research and outreach activities around Mixe language, history, and culture. She has an undergraduate degree in Hispanic language and literatures and a master's in linguistics, both from the Universidad Nacional Autónoma de México. She has collaborated in a variety of projects on Indigenous language outreach and documentation of at-risk languages. She has been involved in the development of Mixe writing and promoting reading in Mixe and other Indigenous languages. She is an activist for Indigenous language rights and the use of Indigenous languages online and in literary translation.

Daniel Badenes holds a doctorate in social sciences and is professor of history and media at Universidad Nacional de La Plata and Universidad Nacional de Quilmes, where he currently also serves as curriculum coordinator. He has directed more than 30 undergraduate and graduate theses. He is the principal investigator for "La edición en la era de redes" [Publishing in a connected era] and also organizes the "El Sur También Publica" book fair [The South also publishes] since it began in 2011, now counting 120 independent and state-funded publishers each year. He is the editor or autor of *Un pasado para La Plata* (2015), *Editar sin patrón* (2017), *Estado de feria permanente* (2019), *El diario de los chicos* (2022), and *El Estado editor* (2024), among others. He has participated in community and independent media, such as La Pulseada and Radio Futura in La Plata and served as president of the Asociación de Revistas Culturales Independientes de Argentina [Association of Independent Cultural Journals of Argentina, ARECIA], 2013-2014.

Paloma Celis Carbajal serves as the curator for Latin American, Iberian, and U.S. Latine Collections for The New York Public Library (NYPL). She is responsible for the development of the research collections in these areas in the arts, humanities, and social sciences. Prior to joining the NYPL, she served for 14+ years as the bibliographer for Ibero-American studies and Romance languages at the University of Wisconsin-Madison. There she founded and developed the most comprehensive cartonera book collection and database. Her publications include "Cartonera Publishers: Of Cardboard Boxes and Cultural Capital" in *The Routledge Companion to Twentieth and Twenty-First Century Latin American Literary and Cultural Forms* (2022). More details at https://orcid.org/0000-0001-6094-6293

Marc Delcan is an autonomous editor and printer for Ona Ediciones, also distributor with Ona Redistribuidora. Previously he was a bookseller and publisher for La Reci (San Cristóbal de las Casas, Chiapas), and a member of the Pensaré Cartoneras collective. He is the co-author of *Cartonear es camino: Colectivo cartonero, autónomo anticolonial* [The path is cardboard: Cartonera collectives, anticolonial autonomy] (Pensaré, 2019). Marc holds a master's in humanities from the Universitat Pompeu Fabra (Barcelona) and is currently a Ph.D. candidate at Centro de Estudios Superiores de México y Centroamérica of the Universidad de Ciencias y Artes de Chiapas, working on colonial continuums in the cultural industry.

Lisa Gardinier is the curator for international literature at the University of Iowa Libraries. She has published on Latin American collections in U.S. libraries in the *Journal of Academic Librarianship* and *College & Research Libraries*. She holds master's degrees in library science from Indiana University and Latin American studies from the University of Arizona.

paul holzman is a homemaker, musician, translator, customer support representative, and printmaker. He has lived in Buenos Aires, Argentina, for over 15 years and is originally from North America. His practice focuses on the art of the cottage industry, revolving around a homemade proofing press and studio; making zines, pamphlets, sounds and small print objects.

Kathia Salomé Ibacache Oliva is the Romance languages librarian at the University of Colorado, Boulder. As a subject specialist, she is interested in advancing diverse collections in Romance and Indigenous languages. Her research interest encompasses digital accessibility within teaching and learning technologies, collection development, and representing Latin American Indigenous language materials in university libraries. Kathia won an IMPART Award in 2019 and is currently an associate professor. Kathia holds a M.L.I.S. degree from San José State University and a Doctor of Musical Arts degree from the University of Southern California.

María José Montezuma Jaramillo holds an undergraduate degree in language and literature education from the Universidad Antonio Ruiz de Montoya and a masters in Hispanic American literature from the Pontificia Universidad Católica de Perú. She has experience as an editor, literature researcher, and facilitator of reading and writing. She has given workshops on zines, cartonera books, and creative writing for children, teens, and adults. She was part of La Ingeniosa Cartonera for 10 years, publishing cartonera books written by students. Since 2018, she is the co-founder of Diversa Cartonera, a press dedicated to promoting and democratizing dissident literature.

Idalia Morejón Arnaiz is professor of Hispanic American literatura at the Universidade de São Paulo (USP). She is author of *Política y polémica en América Latina. Las revistas Casa de las Américas y Mundo Nuevo* (2010) and co-editor of *Escenas del yo flotante. Cuba: escrituras autobiográficas* (2017). She is the director of Malha Fina Cartonera, based in the Faculdade de Filosofia, Letras e Ciências Humanas at USP.

Chayenne Orru Mubarack is a doctoral researcher in the Programa de Pós-Graduação em Língua Espanhola e Literaturas Espanhola e Hispano-Americana at the Universidade de São Paulo. She is a Spanish teacher who has worked in both public and private instruction in São Paulo. She is a member of Malha Fina Cartonera since its foundation and has been involved in book production, translation, and editing.

gaita nihil is a trans cultural woker, poet, and publisher. He is director of puntos suspensivos ediciones, a independent press in Buenos Aires publishing LGBTQ authors. He studied philosophy and publishing at the Universidad de Buenos Aires and has a postgraduate degree (2023) in cultural management and communication from Facultad Latinoamericana de Ciencias Sociales (FLACSO). He is currently purisng a diploma in cultural mediation through the Consejo Latinoamericano de Ciencias Sociales. He is the author of four books of poetry and organized the first festival of trans poetry. He curated the art series LGTB+ No es un secreto in the Centro Cultural de

España en Buenos Aires and has produces music and poetry events on sex and gender dissidences. He contributes to the *Soy* supplement of the *Página 12* newspaper.

Jack Rockwell is a literary translator, writer, and editor. His translation of Julia Kornberg's Berlin Atomized was published by Astra House in December 2024. Other work has appeared in *North American Review*, *The Chicago Review of Books*, *Words Without Borders*, *The Rumpus*, *Latin American Literature Today*, and elsewhere. He holds a M.F.A. in literary translation from the University of Iowa.

Eric Schierloh is an author, editor, and publisher. Since 2010, he directs the artesanal press Barba de Abejas, and regularly teaches "Print or Die!" workshops on self-publishing and artesanal publishing. His recent publications include a compilation and translation of Virginia Woolf's writings on Hogarth Press, *Dedos de coliflor: Diario de una editora artesanal* (2023), *¿ISBN? No gracias* (2023), *Lo obsoleto* (2022), *Manual de edición artesanal* (2022), and *La escritura aumentada* (2021). Find him on Instagram @barbadeabejas.

Rosa Serna is a translator, editor, and publisher. She founded Ediciones Invertidas, an autonomous press publishing women's and dissident voices. Serna believes publishing to be a creative space for construction, meeting, and listening, but is also on the front lines of resistance and creating possibilities. She cofound La Enredadera cultural space in San Cristóbal de las Casas, Chiapas, which includes Ediciones Invertidas within its publishing workspace and in-house library. La Enredadera is conceived as a space to meet, read, and share books on dissidence, anticapitalism, decoloniality, feminism, resistance, well-being, and general trickery, through presentations, workshops, music, exhibitions, films, and other activities. Serna pursued a masters in feminist studies and interventions at the Centro de Estudios Superiores de México y Centroamérica of the Universidad de Ciencias y Artes de Chiapas. She is always exploring and learning other ways of making a more livable present.

Pacelli Dias Alves de Sousa is a doctoral researcher in the Programa de Pós-Graduação em Língua Espanhola e Literaturas Espanhola e Hispano-Americana at the Universidade de São Paulo and the Instituto de Literatura Hispanoamericana at the Universidad de Buenos Aires. His current research focus is children's memories in Latin American literature. He is a member of Malha Fina Cartonera since its foundation, for which he has served multiple roles.

Terezinha de Fátima Carvalho de Souza has a doctorate in information science from Universidade Federal de Minas Gerais (UFMG). She has carried out research in the areas of business information, information sources, and information archeology. She is an associate professor at the UFMG School of Information Science, which she also served as director, 2017-2021. She was the editor of *Perspectivas em Ciência da Informação* from 2013 to 2023, and is currently honorary editor. She is also a former editor of *Múltiplos Olhares em Ciência da Informação* (2011-2018) and coordinator of the Management Committee of the UFMG Periodicals Portal (2019-2023). She is interested in the areas of information management, analysis and dissemination, scientific communication, publishing, and discourse analysis.

Allison Stickley has a M.F.A. in literary translation and a M.A. in Spanish literature from the University of Iowa, where she is currently pursuing a Ph.D. in Spanish literature with a certificate in book arts. Her translations have been published in *The Scores* and by Oomph! Press, as well as by local zines and independent publications in Iowa City.

Peter Tanner (he, él, ele) is associate instructor of Spanish–Bridge Program, at the University of Utah and editor of *Openings: Studies in Book Art*, the journal of the College Book Art Association. His research focuses on artist books from Latin America. He has presented on artist books and book art theory in multiple conferences and published articles on artist books, including connections between William Morris and the Latin American Boom and the artist book as archive. He is currently working on several articles involving artist books that include canonical vanguard authors from Latin America. He has a Ph.D. in Spanish, a M.A. in Latin American art history, and a B.F.A. in painting and printing.

E Tonatiuh Trejo has a degree in graphic communication from the Facultad de Artes y Diseño of the Universidad Nacional Autónoma de México (UNAM) and continuing education in visual studies at 17, Instituto de Estudios Críticos. He is the founder, editor, and designer of Laboratorio Editorial Esto es un Libro, a publishing project of exploration and reflection on the publishing process. He is also the founder and director of the Biblioteca de Anomalías Editoriales and co-founder of the bookstore El Anhelo: Libros Libres de Latinoamérica in Oaxaca. He was an editor for Revista Sensacional de Cineastas (UNAM) and co-founded Librería K in the Casa Refugio Citlaltépetl (Mexico City).

Gustavo Velázquez holds an undergraduate degree in social communication and a master's in cultural industry, both from the Universidad Nacional de Quilmes (Argentina). He is part of the outreach project "El sur también publica" [The south also publishes] and the research project "La edición en la era de las redes" [Publishing in a connected era], both based at UNQ. He has contributed to edited volumes *Estado de feria permanente* (2019) and *El Estado editor* (2024). He is currently pursing a doctorate in social and human sciences at UNQ, with a dissertation on distribution strategies of independent publishers in the Buenos Aires metropolitan área. His work is supported by the Consejo Nacional de Investigaciones Científicas y Técnicas (CONICET).

David Woken is the Latin American and Caribbean Studies librarian at the University of Chicago Library. He has published on critical pedagogy methods with historical primary source materials and U.S. farmworker history, and is currently working as co-principal investigator on a digital scholarship project to preserve Mesoamerican-language materials held at the University of Chicago. He holds master's degrees in Latin American history from Indiana University and library and information studies from the University of Wisconsin-Madison.

Index

academic libraries. *See* libraries, academic
Aguilar Gil, Yásnaya, 13-18, 199
alternative publishing. *See* publishing, alternative
Amorosa y Rebelde Red de Editoriales, 75
anti-racism, 4, 73-74
Argentine publishing. *See* publishing, Argentine
ARRE. *See* Amorosa y Rebelde Red de Editoriales
artisanal publishing. *See* publishing, artisanal
artist books
  definition of, 139-140, 141, 156
  examples of, 157-162
  history of, 140-148,156
  in Latin America, 8, 139-140, 152-156
  in the Americas, 140-148
Asunto Impreso, 50

Badenes, Daniel, 199
bibliodiversity, 41-43, 167-168, 174, 178-182
Bicha Trava Publishing, 81
book catalogs, 40
book fairs, 7, 52, 58-61, 92-93, 127
book sales, 49, 125-128
Brazilian publishing. *See* publishing, Brazilian

Carbono, 50, 57
Cartonera, Eloisa, 8, 113-115, 166
cartonera publishing. *See* publishing, cartonera
case studies, 7-8
Celis Carbajal, Paloma, 200
collaboration, 7, 49
collaborative distribution. *See* distribution, collaborative
colonialism, 5
commercialization, 50, 85-86
Como Cuatro, 50, 52, 53
cultural capital, 100-102

decolonization, 4

Delcan, Marc, 200
digital publishing. *See* publishing, digital
distribution, 50, 56-58, 60-61, 91-92
distribution, collaborative, 7, 49-50
distribution, mixed character, 55
distribution, self, 50-51
distribution, third party, 50-52
DIY publishing. *See* publishing, DIY

English language, 18

FEA. *See* Feminismos, Estrias y Autogestió
feminism, 7, 73-74
Feminismos, Estrias y Autogestió, 80
Feria del Libro Independiente, 7, 35-36
Fixed Price Law, 88, 93-94
FLIA. *See* Feria del Libro Independiente
Frente Mar, 50, 60-61
Furia del Libro, 7, 63, 64

Gardinier, Lisa, 200

hegemony, 87
holzman, paul, 200

Ibacache Oliva, Kathia Salomé, 200-201
independent publishing. *See* publishing, independent
industrial publishing. *See* publishing, industrial
Ingeniosa Cartonera, 8-9

La Coop, 50, 53-54
La Ingeniosa Cartonera, 168-174
La IngeniosaTruequeferia, 174-177
Latin American Indigenous language materials. *See* library materials, Latin American Indigenous language
Latin American library materials. *See* library materials, Latin American
Latin American publishing. *See* publishing, Latin American
libraries, academic, 1-2, 106-110

library materials, Latin American, 1-2
library materials, Latin American
 Indigenous language, 102-106
LIBRE. *See* Liga Brasileira de Editoras
Liga Brasileira de Editoras, 88
literacy, 5, 13-18

Malha Fina Cartonera
 as outreach laboratory, 128-136
 book sales for, 125-128
 description of, 8
 establishment of, 113-120
 history of, 113-125
 major goals of, 8, 136-137
 participation in book fairs, 127
 spread of, 113-120
Malisia, 50, 54-56
Mariposa Cartonera, 116
Mexican publishing. *See* publishing,
 Mexican
Mixe language, 14, 16-18
mixed character distribution. *See*
 distribution, mixed character
Montezuma Jaramillo, María José, 201
Morejón Arnaiz, Idalia, 201
Mubarack, Chayenne Orru, 201

nihil, gaita, 201-202

Pensaré Cartoneras, 75
Peruvian publishing. *See* publishing,
 Peruvian
print culture, 6-7
publishing, Argentine, 6-7, 30-32
publishing, alternative, 1-3, 9
publishing, artisanal, 8-9, 22, 23-24
publishing, Brazilian, 7-8, 87-94
publishing, cartonera
 characteristics of, 8-9, 165-166
 definition of, 8, 165
 establishment of, 165-166
 history of, 8-9
 in Brazil, 116
 in Peru, 165-167
 in scholastic environments, 8-9, 165-167
 objectives of, 136-137
 spread of, 8
publishing, digital, 67-69
publishing, DIY, 67-69
publishing, independent
 as antagonist to economic concentration,
 38-40
 as catalog project, 40-46
 characteristics of, 32-33, 37, 63-64
 definition of, 32-33, 37, 63-64
 effects of economic globalization on, 43
 history of, 27-30
publishing, industrial, 7, 21-25
publishing, Latin American, 1-9
publishing, Mexican, 9, 189
publishing, Peruvian, 165-167
publishing, self, 189

puntos suspensivos ediciones, 67-69

queer communities, 7, 67-69

reading, 6-7, 9, 13-18
Riot Grrrl, 77-78
Rockwell, Jack, 202

Schierloh, Eric, 202
self distribution. *See* distribution, self
self publishing. *See* publishing, self
Serna, Rosa, 71-72, 202
silence, 3-4
social capital, 97-100
Sousa, Pacelli Dias Alves de, 202
Souza, Terezinha de Fátima Carvalho de, 203
Spanish language, 14-15, 18
Stickley, Allison, 203

Taller Leñateros, 148-152
Tanner, Peter, 203
Textura Fair, 89
third party distribution. *See* distribution,
 third party
Todo Libro es Politico, 50, 58-60
Trejo, E Tonatiuh, 185-189, 191-192, 195, 203
Trouillot, Michel-Rolph, 3

Velázquez, Gustavo, 204
Videos de Recomendaciones Bibliodiversas,
 174, 178-180

Woken, David, 204

Yiyi Jambo, 116

zines, 76-79

www.ingramcontent.com/pod-product-compliance
Lightning Source LLC
Chambersburg PA
CBHW050302010526
44108CB00040B/2054